AF477342

THE COSMIC WAY OF MANKIND

THE COSMIC WAY OF MANKIND

K. O. Schmidt

Translated by: Léone Muller

CSA Press
Lakemont, Georgia 30552

CONTENTS

Foreword to the First American Edition

K.O. Schmidt in this new American Edition of THE
COSMIC WAY OF MANKIND expands the consciousness of modern man through his brilliant use of
language in explicating ideas that to most of us have been
undecipherable. We have all, at one time or another,
thought of the possibility of estraterrestrial life and civilization being extant and imminent—existing and occur-
ring within the boundaries of the infinite universe. The
author enables the reader to define and realize the reality
of such forms and cultures while delineating the possibilities of man having reached his present state of being re-
sultant from past contact with other forms, other lands,
other times.

There is no demise of existence or a going-on of life
and form according to Schmidt but simply a continuum
of the all. He says that astrosophy and cosmobiology tie
in with the wisdom of the astromants of civilizations that
vanished long ago. There is the probability that empathy

was attained and positive adaptation to cosmic energy flows, energy radiations, rhythms and laws, not in secondary ways—through intellectual speculation—but in primary ways—through meditative contemplation of the universe and intuitive understanding of Reality were also made available to the ever-evolving life and form of the time. Through this gift of enlightenment man has been put into an advantageous position allowing him to experience that feeling of absolute security which goes far beyond the next feeling of being under a protective roof, in the bosom of one's family, of a religious or political community, or a people, and by which alone man will be able to master more extended space travel without space fear!

We are told that only a few individuals have reached cosmic maturity. We, today, are only at the beginning of the cosmic age, getting closer to understanding the mystery of life and being able to fathom that it is older than the stars. Matter is only another form of energy which, being tangible to our reception, allows us as questers needing to decipher the idea of the eternal, further clues to the dilemma of existence.

In a quotation from Paracelsus we learn that philosophy does not find anything in the entire cosmos that it does not also find in man. For the hand of Him Who created heaven and earth has also created the microcosm. That is why the external heaven is a signpost for us to the inner, and the inner, a gate to the universe. This thought, so eloquently and simply stated in the original, seems to say that we have been given the key to unlock the door that leads onto the path of unending knowing of one's self that in turn is the solution to the ultimate realization of the universe. The sad and certainly unfortunate aspect of trying to define the revelation of reality is the necessity for an eternal divisibility of the realm of the cognitive. The author has overcome this inherent fallacy of logic through consistent focus of thought.

Each of our tasks in life is infinite as we travel through the dynamic cosmos which has been carefully planned as an orderly system that is Spirit-permeated, hierarchically structured into a harmonious whole behind whose manifoldness there lies an ultimate oneness. Though we are microbelike, infinitesimal dwellers on this planet earth which is located in one of the one-hundred billion solar systems of our galaxy, the Milky Way, we are gifted with the ability to apprehend the nature and shape of the universe by means of instruments created by us. We can deduce from the light of the stars and nebulae their inner structure and realize our own position in the universe proving that the Universal Soul itself dwells within us knowing that we are truly children of the universe.

In meditative All-reflection we pass from the usual cosmic analysis, as is done by astronomy and astrophysics, to cosmosynthesis which is the vision of the total unity of the world process. In this process we touch upon the meaning of the whole and the spiritual unity behind the diversity of appearances. This "touching" brings us ever closer to the reality of the oneness but does not in itself allow for synonymity or a dissolution of the self into the one. There is always, regardless of how we try to define or express the idea, the ever-present reality of an existing duality. In this very duality lies the flaw that hinders our progress toward the attainment of oneness. Even in the word, oneness, the duality inherent in the process of defining is there to thwart the realization of the revelation. Always it is our lot to be thrust back into the cognitive in our unending quest to experience oneness with the all. The fallacy is the need to define the knowing, the revelation. A going inward to the source of the self rather than a flowing outward may seem to some the solution to the enigma of existence, but in reality there is the need to eliminate in our very makeups the idea of an existing polarity before the realization of the revelation as an experience of reality can be known. There can literally be no "in's" and no "out's" or ups-downs, blacks-whites, hots-colds, etc. for any individual to learn the knowing experience of oneness.

In experiencing the idea of oneness, death has lost its sting. Finally the childhood stage is overcome and an understanding that home is a star among stars has been realized. Though there will probably always be an element of humanity that lives within the antlike delusion that the Earth is the only inhabited body in space and human beings are the "only elect of God," let us not forget that there are also beings in other worlds whose self-over-estimation is proportionate to the limitation of their intellectual capacity and who consider themselves the only thinking beings in the universe.

Whether we turn inward or outward, if the idea of polarity persists toward the universe, ultimately we attain the same realization of the All-unity of life. The old hermetic word "As above, so below" is equally valid for the higher dimension, "As within, so without"! The author states that the way of all evolution points from the finite to the infinite, from the temporary to the eternal, from the earthly to the cosmic, and from the human to the divine and beyond. In our efforts to finally become one with the all a full cognizance of this reality is evident and our task of attempting throughout the continuum of life to constantly perfect all living things becomes the logical answer to the quest.

In this marvelous treatise that gives the reader the unique opportunity to expand his consciousness, K.O. Schmidt, the master metaphysician, closes with a most prophetic statement, "When the 'Omega Point' is attained, it is simultaneously an 'Alpha Point.' It is the beginning of a new metacosmic evolution, which may well include myriad times more wonders than the cosmic evolutionary levels from primitive man to the Godman, leading beyond the cosmocrats and divine beings into the blazing All-heart of the universal Godhead." Finally he says that man sees revealed that God is love and that love is God.

R. Hunter Brannan
Lake Rabun—1975

THE
COSMIC WAY
OF
MANKIND

FROM THE VANTAGE POINT
OF THE AQUARIAN AGE

"Men forget and despair only too often, otherwise they would find that the perception and trust in the divine laws of the great world process can more easily predict the goal than a wealth of knowledge of political events is able to."

Jean Paul

I. *Astrology and Astrosophy*

If we consider the events of today and tomorrow from the higher, the mental-energetic, vantage point of the Aquarian Age, in the dawn of which we are living, we clearly perceive certain facts and consequences which are also significant and useful for our present life and conduct.

Included in these is the realization that we human beings are not only children of the Earth but, to a far greater extent than we have been aware of until now, children of the sun and the cosmos.

A second realization is that the belief in the stars of the ancient civilizations, if it is stripped of all later accretions, rests upon an intuitive sensing of the spiritual unity of the universe, of the "divine laws of the great world process" and the dynamic relatedness of all life to the totality of cosmic happenings. This does not only apply to life on our small planet but to all worlds of the physical universe and the higher-dimensional regions.

Details of these and other universal insights lying at the root of the ancient wisdom of the stars have been partly confirmed by astronomy and partly disputed and rejected.

Today, in the era of beginning space travel and the expansion of consciousness into the universal, both are beginning to unite as *astrosophy* and *cosmobiology* in realistic stellar wisdom and the realization of the unity of all life. This takes place to the extent that intuition turns into knowledge and conjecture into certainty.

The first rudiments of this development are already noticeable.

We know of the varied energetic influences of the *sun* upon earthly life and happenings. It is well known that the sun's own 27-day rotation affects the atmospheric conditions and the state of organisms on the Earth. Likewise, that solar eruptions and the energy flows of the sun cause corresponding disturbances both in the Earth's electromagnetic field and the bioelectric potential of living beings, especially men.

Even before the turn of the century, the physical chemist *Svante Arrhenius* dealth with questions of "the impact of cosmic influences upon physiological conditions."

Later. medical doctors, among others, *B. Duell* (in "Virchows Archiv" 34), reported about the "dependence of the state of health on sudden solar eruptions'' and the "existence of a 27-day rhythm in death.''

Since that time statistics have shed more light on the relation between solar activity and terrestrial weather, the quantity of rainfall, the width of the annual rings of trees and the appearance of rheumatism and infectious diseases.

It is less known that the frequency of marriages, the development of prices and other economic factors are also influenced by sunspot activity.

The *lunar* phases, too, are influencing the tides, the weather and biological processes in many different ways. It is needless to quote examples. We would only mention that births frequently take place at flood or ebb tides, which shows how far-reaching complex biological processes run parallel with the change of tides.

The influence of *cosmic rays* upon terrestrial events and life is today also the subject of research. It is undeniable that we are far more influenced by cosmic rhythms than we had thought possible until now.

Even if we human beings—seen from outside—are but one of innumerable life forms on the crust of a tiny planet of a small sun in one of the outer spiral arms of our Milky Way or galaxy, we are simultaneously—seen from inside—*children of the cosmos* and destined to cosmic unfoldment according to our predispositions and abilities.

Our Earth is only the planetary nursery, which we leave for the first time (spiritually as well as physically) in the Aquarian Age in order to attain cosmic maturity in the course of our further development.

This realization had already been obtained by the astromants of cultures that have long since vanished, and it can today be obtained by ourselves on the way inward.

The astromants knew—and we can sense it in retrospective meditation—that nothing in life is due to chance, but that everything is subject to destiny-shaping laws.

They operate from the day we are born, since we do not enter existence as a blank page but as the recipient of a rich heritage from previous lives—including the positive and negative attachments we then formed to other beings, that is, to other energy fields.

Viewed from that standpoint, the moment of *birth* is the point of crystallization of the balance of man's destiny-account, his karma. It is that part of his karma that has become active, striving for manifestation. Through countless energy flows it is causally connected with the destinies of other beings as well as with the collective destiny of mankind.

Just how that karma will take effect in life depends of course on man's present mental attitude, conduct and actions. It is always up to him what he wants to make of himself and his destiny.

Such was one of the fundamental ideas contained in the wisdom of the ancient astromants, the knowledge of which can throw light on the future.

II. *Astromants—Astronauts from Distant Worlds?*

Astrosophy and cosmobiology tie in with the wisdom of the astromants of civilizations that vanished long ago. They attained empathy and positive adaptation to cosmic energy flows, energy radiations, rhythms and laws, not in secondary ways—through intellectual speculation—but in primary ways—through meditative contemplation of the universe and intuitive understanding of Reality.

Through their vivid sense of harmony with the universe they developed the ability to survey the destinies of men, for which the changing motion of the stars took on a symbolic character.

Simultaneously, there grew within them something that man will again enjoy to the full in the Aquarian Age: that feeling of absolute security which goes far beyond the nest feeling of being under a protective roof, in the bosom of one's family, of a religious or political community, or a people, and by which alone man will be able to master more extended space travel without space fear.

We know little about the origin of the cosmic wisdom of the astromants of prehistoric times.

Did they have a radarlike ability to feel at a distance, which they directed at cosmic force fields and mental impulses of inhabited regions of far-away stellar worlds, and has that ability since shriveled up? Or did they draw their knowledge from contacts with cosmic foreign visitors, with cosmonauts from distant solar realms—or were they themselves such cosmonauts?

It is food for thought that similar representations of the motion of the sun through the twelve space force fields of the zodiac can be found among ancient peoples of the East and West, which can hardly be explained in view of the absence or deficiency of continental communications in those times.

And how can we explain that the measurements of the exactly 5,000 year old Cheops pyramid contain more mathematical and astronomical data than have been known until today?

Many other findings, but also the myths and legends of the Ancients, allow us to assume that there existed advanced civilizations on earth long before our era and that we hardly know anything about them.

It has for some time been asked whether those former advanced civilizations did not perhpas have their origin in visits from more highly developed entities from distant worlds, who appeared to primitive men to be angels or gods.

What, for instance, do we know of the "Vimanas," of which the Mahabharata and other ancient Indian epics report that they expelled streams of fire when rising up to heaven?

Were they rocketlike spacecraft—relics of a lost civilization which had already advanced to the stage where it knew how to release atomic energies, and then destroyed itself? Or were those "Vimanas" spacecraft of cosmic visitors who landed on earth, mixed with men and left the Earth again?

What do we know of the origin of man and whether perhaps his ancestors came from one of those stars to which we look up full of longing?

To what extent are the legends of the Ancients about gods and angels faded and corrupted memories of spiritually and technically more highly developed entities from other stellar realms, who also visited the Earth in the course of their space travels and gave to man a little of their cosmic knowledge, thus ushering in a new epoch in the development of mankind?

Everything points to the fact that these questions will receive an answer in the aeon of Aquarius which would be baffling to us today but will be accepted as a matter of course in the future.

In this connection, we may ask what is the real significance of the "Aquarian Age," which is so much talked about, although little concrete information is given about it.

III. *End of the Era of Pisces*

Mankind is today standing at a portentous turning of the times, in a transitional period between two eras: the end of the era of "Pisces" and the ascending of the aeon of "Aquarius."

Its unmistakable mark is the stormy development of the ever stronger "metaphysical unrest." Depending upon their spiritual attitude and maturity, men either become insecure and unstable within, or they are spurred on to break through to self-recollection and reliance upon their inner strength.

The political and social unrest throughout the world is but the mass-biological equivalent of people's inner restlessness.

Contact with the vibrations of the New Age triggers new insights and perceptions in inwardly awakened persons, while causing existential fear, flight into materialism or sectarianism, in the unawakened. At all turning points of history sectarianism grows stronger, leading to a fear-centered superstitious belief in an "end of the times" with the corresponding end-of-the-world visions smouldering in the collective unconscious.

Because the "old man" still anchored in the Age of Pisces sees but one side of the process, he misinterpets the "end of the times," which is in reality a change of the times.

Indeed, man is not at the end of his career but *at the beginning of an evolution covering millions of years*. It is leading him upward from egocentric man to superman, from there to spiritual man and further on to the level of Allman or Godman—to dimensions of consciousness of which cosmic consciousness is only a first step.

The current stormy period is meant to serve the separation of minds: Some cling to matter and go in this life the way of all perishable things. Others learn to live by the spirit, becoming ever more conscious of their cosmic destination and evolution.

That explains why they turn their eyes away from the Earth to the universe and simultaneously to the inner universe, the Inner-All.

In the midst of the transience of their self-centered existence, they feel increasingly the breath of eternity of their inner nucleus, their Self.

They become receptive for the mental and spiritual vibrations and energy flows of the new aeon, indicated by the symbol of Aquarius.

They develop a feel for the grand vision of those cosmic eras which the astromants of long ago described.

The average man of today thinks in minute periods of time, which go hardly further back than the 6,000 years of biblical chronology or the few million years of modern biology.

Let us compare those figures with the *cosmic chronology* of the Brahmanic astromants who assigned 432,000 years to the now ending era of "Kali-Yuga."

That amounts to one-tenth of the greater chronological circle of "Maha-Yuga," comprising 4,320,000 years.

But only a thousand Maha-Yugas form a *"Kalpa"* or *"day of Brahma"* (4,320,000,000), to which is added an equally long "night of Brahma," together 8,64 billion years.

One *"year of Brahma"* in turn lasts 3,11 trillion years, while a *"Maha-Kalpa"*—a metacosmic world-day of one hundred years of Brahma—covers 311 trillion years, etc. . . . .

The classification of those periods comprises a multiplicity of cosmic evolutionary cycles which we need not discuss further here.

In this context we are only interested in the fact that "Satya-Yuga" is approaching—the Golden Age of the former evolutionary spiral.

We are even more interested in the statement of the astromants that the end of the "Kali-Yuga" is marked by the prevalence of selfish-commercial thinking. Not only does this mentality consider work and human achievement, but man himself and all life, as a usable commodity, and it tries to exploit man and the universe to the last atom.

Is there a more fitting definition of the materialist mentality of the last 5,000 years of history, especially of the Age of Pisces, also the age of "swimming" through a growing tide of mental and political ideologies and philosophies of life, creeds and religions?

And is there a more comforting promise than that this epoch of self-centered utilitarianism will be followed by a wise realization of Reality on a universal scale—an age of mutual respect, tolerance and friendship, reciprocal assistance, harmony and unity?

IV. *Beginning the Age of Aquarius*

In answer to the question *when* the brighter Age of Aquarius began or begins, there is no definite reply as to the year and day.

What has been said previously in this connection is extrapolation, as statisticians call the inference to a future course from laws within an already observed development.

The fact that those calculations are based on different assumptions explains the difference between the dates quoted, which go from 1900 and before to the year 2000.

Some readers may recall that in 1961 the beginning of the Aquarian Age was said to be February 4, 1962 and that a cosmic catastrophe had been predicted because of the conjunction of the sun, the moon and five planets in Aquarius. Even a "reversal of the rotation of the Earth, a shifting of the poles and disturbances in the planetary orbits" were predicted, although there was no astrophysical justification for it.

What an excitement was stirred up by those amateurish "predictions" which made people flee to supposedly safer areas! The "end of the world" catastrophe took place just as little as did those predicted previously.

Actually, it is a mistake to try to determine the exact time of the beginning of an era, as we are dealing with gradual transitions covering hundreds of years, and which are noticed only by those whose vision reaches beyond the garden fences of their time and society.

To this we may add that the constellations are not fixed, since they consist of suns which pursue their course in the universe with varying degrees of velocity and have changed position since the days when astrology and astronomy developed from the astromancy of the ancient peoples.

What is fixed is the *precession:* the motion of the rotation axis of the spinning top "Earth" around the pole of the ecliptic in 25,800 years, as a consequence of which the beginning of spring moves forward every 70 years by one degree.

This period of 25,800 years is called a "Platonic year," which may be divided into 12 world-months of an average of 2,160 years.

The Aquarius-month, at the beginning of which we are living, also covers that period approximately. It is arbitrary, however, in so far as the individual force fields of the zodiac differ in size and the transitional periods differ in length.

Instead, the beginning of the Aquarian aeon can more easily be pinpointed by its mental influence.

There is a significant symbolism in the fact that this epoch has always been characterized as dominated by *Uranus* and symbolized by a man pouring water onto the earth from a pitcher.

For "water" stands for spirit, and the symbol of Aquarius points to the outpouring of spirit and the *domination of spirit over matter.*

The utilization of atomic energy ushered in by the discovery of *uranium* is but an attendant phenomenon— the material equivalent of the ability characteristic of the Aquarian type to develop and utilize the atomic energies of the soul in the service of human unfoldment from the Earth to the cosmic, and the spirit of unity awakening in mankind.

The Aquarian type, the "New Man" of Modern Age, who is already partly living among us today, also differs from the "old man" of the Piscean Age in that he is not under the influence of history. To him inner happenings and spiritual progress are more important than visible history, under the many layers of which the background elements are often so completely buried that they can only be recognized by those who look deeper.

The "old man" considers it a matter of historical importance that a tribal chief or a commander-in-chief wins battles or wars, while he underestimates an individual's breakthrough to the Inner Light and higher levels of consciousness, which may well determine the fate of millennia.

And since he does not perceive the essential, he tries to safeguard and save himself in every manner.

He does not, however, think of making himself worthy to be saved and of looking for security in his own inner being. Nor does he think of forestalling external upheavals through his own inner transformation and in that way become ready to cope with all external storms.

And yet, the only security we have consists in adopting a new dynamic way of thinking, in the spiritual regeneration and "transmutation" of the old man into the new one.

V. *The Spirit of Aquarius.*

Of course, the "New Men," the Aquarius types, are now only a minority. But they have already made sure that each of us, on the way inward, can become resonant and receptive for the vibrations and dynamic impulses of the New Age.

That insight is necessary, because the "old man" possesses neither the maturity nor the ability to take positive decisions in the name of humanity.

Seen from that vantage point, he has not yet gone beyond the childhood stage, and only individual representatives of the species "homo sapiens," precisely the New Men, are older and more mature and, as awakening men, already part adult and equal to their destiny. Those who are spiritually children may believe that a few unrestrained politicians could destroy mankind by the famous "pushing the button."

The spiritually adult know that the universe in which we are living is governed and directed by very wise powers which the small human *hybris* cannot influence.

Today, the "old man" is trying to build a bridge from the Earth into space, although he is unable to determine the atmospheric and seismological processes on our planet, let alone to control himself and live in peace with his neighbors. Soviet astronauts did not bring back a higher spiritual gain from their space flights than the statement that they "found neither God nor heaven above there in space." All this goes to prove how little the old man is able to think cosmically.

As long, however, as this first prerequisite is lacking and as long as the Earth is still a place of need, misery and unspeakable torment for millions of sentient beings, men and animals, all contact with the mental force fields of progressive cosmic worlds remains blocked. Such contacts were enjoyed by some isolated astromants thousands of years ago and they will be granted in the Cosmic Age to that bold, high-minded, worthy-of-power type of human being who takes the step from egocentric man to *superman* through instrospection and gradual self-realization.

In the New Age, the humanly thinking and feeling man will hold a central position despite all progress in technology, cybernetics and psychodynamics.

He is master of the external world, because he is grounded in the inner world. He knows that heaven is within himself, and with it all the power he needs to walk the path of self-completion, unconcerned with external changes.

But a man may even today be touched and filled by the spirit of the Aquarian aeon if he thinks about himself and, conscious of his total responsibility, recognizes and accepts himself as a test-field and germinal center of the New Man.

He realizes that the overcoming of matter and gravity begins with the new age of the spirit, not only by rockets, satellites and spaceships, but through the spirit.

He knows that spirit is the cause of all things and conditions; matter only chained energy, formed and pervaded, moved and transformed by the creative Spirit.

The two waves of the symbol of Aquarius also point to that fact: They indicate that those who go inward transform matter into spirit and spirit into matter.

As the visionary poet *Hans Sterneder* realized, in the Aquarian Age "the spiritual fire of the Christ force in man begins to burst through the fetters of matter. Atheists and materialists cannot bear that ray of spiritual fire of the New Age but will die of it as of a contagious disease. Those who are spirit-oriented, however, will completely recover under that ray, gather strength and be carried upward to their transformation."

VI. *A New Model of the World*

> "Time is a flowering field,
> Nature is a great living thing,
> And all is fruit, and all is seed."
>
> Schiller

The history of mankind is a history of growing consciousness, of constant expansion of the spiritual and mental, microcosmic and macrocosmic fields of vision, where progress is not added but raised to a higher power.

In the Aquarian Age, that progress will receive new impulses, first and foremost through a change to dynamic vision.

The evaluation of all events in the universe and all vital processes will take place from the vantage point of energetics: they will be recognized as the expression and effect of forces regulated and directed cybernetically by hierarchically graded spiritual powers.

At the start, man took himself, then his village, his country, the Earth, and finally the sun to be the center of the universe. He resembled a man walking through fog, recognizing clearly only what is nearest to him, and everything else the more indistinctly, the farther away it is.

But meanwhile the fog has cleared, and the anthropocentric, geocentric and heliocentric views are making way for cosmocentric insights which will steadily expand in the Aquarian aeon.

We know that the "yellow dwarf," which we call our sun, with its planet children and moon satellites belongs to one of the outer spiral arms of our "Milky Way," which, in addition, has few stars.

We know that the sun is rotating around the center of our galaxy at a distance of approximately 40,000 light-years and at a speed of nearly 1,000,000 miles an hour, requiring about 200,000,000 years to make a round trip of the galaxy.

In his *Theory of Heaven* Immanuel *Kant* was first to consider the cosmic nebulae and "far distant independent systems of stars like our Milky Way." We now realize much more clearly that our home galaxy or "Milky Way," which comprises about 100 billion suns, is only *one* of innumerable billions of similar galaxies or spiral nebulae in the known cosmic space, and we are to think of them as spherical.

We feel already that this cosmic All-space, accessible to us and simultaneously expanding explosively, with a radius of about 100 billion light-years, is but one of myriads of similar universes which, in turn, may form an unimaginably gigantic metacosmos—and so forth.

The fact that we humans are able to think cosmically, to form a realistic idea of the structure of the universe and, in addition, to become conscious of our unity with the universal life and Spirit, shows once again that we are not only creatures of the Earth but children of the cosmos according to our inmost nature.

We know that everywhere in the universe as on our Earth, we have to deal with *force fields,* from those of atoms and living organisms to those of planets, suns and galaxies. They are cybernetically directed units which, with similar and larger units, form a *cosmic whole.*

And we are even today not just feeling like a star among stars, but are beginning to ascend to the constellations.

VII. *Departure for the Universe*

Modern man, in Goethe's words, has "his feet firmly planted on the well-founded Earth," but at the same time his spirit "rises upward and touches the stars."

Our astronauts have already familiarized themselves with the living conditions in space.

They have proved that the human organism can exist in the absence of gravitation.

Space medicine had had doubts about the effect of weightlessness and had also in other respects underestimated human adaptability: Man is evidently built to adapt some day to the totally different environmental factors and conditions of life prevailing on other planets and to develop new senses and organs, powers and abilities in the course of generations through the unfolding of his latent powers of mutation.

Man will also solve the problem of time expansion and contraction in future interstellar space travels, learning to eliminate the disadvantages while making use of the advantages.

Only when this stage has been reached, can we speak of *astronautics.*

In our solar system the Earth is the only planet able

to support human life. All stories about the inhabitants of Venus, Mars and Jupiter are based on wishful thinking which has a semblance of reality only for those who are mentally unstable and suffer from an overdose of imagination.

Since, on the other hand, all suns and planets in space are made of the same elements as our solar system and the Earth, innumerable worlds in the universe offer development possibilities for the most diversified life forms.

Even the cosmic space that can be observed by optical means contains 500 quintillion (5,000,000,000,000,000,000,000) suns, according to estimates by astronomers, of which about one-tenth resemble our sun spectroscopically. Considering only our home galaxy, the Milky Way, we may assume that among its 100 billion suns there are about 10 billion with planetary systems similar to that of our sun. Again, of these at least one percent, that is, 100 million suns, are supposed to be accompanied by planets with similar conditions of life.

We can therefore assume with the astronomer *Harlow Shapely* that in our galaxy living beings of the most different kinds and degrees of maturity have developed on perhaps 100 million earthlike planets during the periods they are inhabitable.*

In so doing, we cannot imagine a large enough diversity of life forms, even if these possibilities are seen within limits determined by cosmological laws and the similarity of chemical elements.

---

*Hoyle, Fred. *The Nature of the Universe,* Basil Blackwell, Oxford 1950: We read on page 21, "When you look at the heavens, how many of the stars you see have planets encircling them and on how many of these planets might living creatures look out on a very similar scene?— To give a numerical estimate I would say that more than a million stars in the Milky Way possess planets on which you might live without undue comfort."

We are justified in inferring that among the billions of creatures in other worlds there are also many who resemble terrestrial life forms.

We should guard, however, against a too earth and time-bound overestimation of those possibilities to which even astronomers are falling victim. As an example, we may quote the director of the observatory for radioastronomy in Jodrell, Banks, Sir Bernhard *Lovell,* who expressed his conviction that there are intelligent living beings on a multiplicity of planets in the universe, of whom many have developed like terrestrial man and who, like ourselves, may be about to extinguish themselves and their worlds in nuclear catastrophes.

It is an all too human thought that our mistakes should be repeated in other worlds.

Indeed, we can agree with Lovell's further statement that many kinds of living beings on other stars may be ahead of us in their development by a hundred thousand or millions of years and that there may also exist beings on other planets who have by far not reached our level of civilization.

VIII. *Life on other worlds*

The examination of meteorites, which have come to us from infinite distances and were a few billion years old when they reached the end of their world travels on the Earth, prove that the organismic structure of alien life forms is also based on protoplasm, although it may assume different forms.

Even in intergalactic clouds of gas and dust astronomical observatories could recently detect simple and more complicated organic compounds, which permits us to conclude that life cells and life forms can also develop in "empty" space, although they may be of a totally different kind than the planetary ones.

Discoveries of meteorites further confirm that countless stars are older than our relatively young sun and that the cultural and technical development of some of their planet dwellers may be ahead of the Earth by millions of years and may be infinitely superior.

Let us never forget that man is only one of quintillions of possible life forms. Even at best, seen from a terrestrial standpoint, the ecological conditions and developmental factors in regard to climate, soil, food, the vegetable and animal kingdoms, etc., are exceedingly varied.

On the other hand, the bodily covers of the dwellers of other worlds—irrespective of whether they have a gaseous, plasmatic, fluid or firm structure—are composed of the same elements as those which form the bodies of the inhabitants of the Earth. Different gravitational forces and other factors may be at work, however, and we may find, for instance, that their bodies require silicon instead of carbon.

Accordingly, their bodily functions follow similar physical and chemical laws to those of terrestrial creatures.

Nevertheless, we should not think in too anthropomorphic terms. "Terraneans," earthmen, breathe oxygen and we feel that our Earth with its manifold opportunities for existence and development and its natural beauties is both suitable for us and pleasant.

Instead, methane breathing creatures could live on our planet as little as we could in their worlds, in the atmosphere of Jupiter, for instance.

We human beings depend on the present combination of temperature, light, air and water. For beings of other worlds the atmosphere or mean surface temperature of the Earth may be deadly.

We human beings have a biologically determined life expectancy and a rate of reaction dependent upon it. Other beings may well live, think and react a hundred times faster or slower, and have a different biological rhythm.

We human beings live on vital food, that is, on other life. Inhabitants of remote worlds, whose energy economy does not depend on the chemical processing of other vital substances, may be able to transform solar energy directly into vital energy. Or they may inhale the vital substances required, absorb them through their bodily covers, or maintain their physical forms in another way.

On this Earth, only a few Saints and Yogis have achieved this. But some day we shall be able to do it too, and not only shall we transform matter into energy as we do today, but also energy into organic matter.

All entities in the universe have one thing in common, *spirit,* and in a more or less developed stage, *mind.*

And since thoughts, seen from the viewpoint of energetics, are psychoelectronic impulses which can also operate at a distance and be intensified by appropriate equipment, in the Aquarian Age we human beings will increasingly learn to switch instruments and machines on and off, to direct and regulate them by remote mental impulses—which may well be a matter of course for more highly developed beings.

Even before that, we may see come to pass what the chemist and recipient of the Nobel prize, H.C. Urey, expected. He said in fact that other intelligent beings on worlds still unknown to us, may well discuss the possibility of life on other planets and that the most marvelous thing one can imagine would be to make contact with them.

IX. *Awakening of the Universal Sense*

What can we human beings do to bring about cosmic contacts with inhabitants of other worlds in the foreseeable future?

The first requirement is for us to learn to think not just planetwise but cosmically, and to acquire that ethical basis which makes us able and ripe first to communicate with entities of other worlds and later to cooperate with them to our mutual benefit.

As we know, some hopes were put on radiotelescopic attempts of American astronomers, such as project OZMA in West Virginia, to intercept radio signals of thinking beings from the relatively close solar systems Tau in "Cetus the Whale" and Epsilon in "Eridanus," over a distance of 11 light-years.

Those hopes have so far not been fulfilled.

But after all, like all technical contrivances, the radiotelescope with its range of billions of light-years is but the material equivalent of a still undeveloped universal telepathic sense inherent in each of us. Once it is activated and correctly tuned, it enables us to make cosmic contacts with mentally like-minded, even if physically different, inhabitants of alien solar realms, opening up such wonders of remote worlds as we are unable to imagine today.

In this connection the situation is about the same as in the riddles of the Hereafter, which are the subject of the famous story of the two monks.

They arranged between themselves that the one who would die first would communicate with the other at least with one word, and they chose the Latin word "taliter" (so, such, of such kind), if the Hereafter did indeed correspond with their mutual ideas about it. They would use "aliter" (otherwise, different), if the reality in the Beyond were different.

When one of the monks manifested to the other after his death, he did so in two words, "Totaliter aliter" (totally different) . . . .

The constitution of life in other worlds may well also prove to be "totaliter aliter" from the descriptions of the fantasies of science fiction writers.

As said before, we acquire a feel for it on the way

inward, there where all living things in the universe are connected psychoenergetically and are spiritually one.

The unfoldment of that sense and the cosmotelepathic contacts made possible through it are a mark of the Aquarian Age.

Some individuals have already had first-hand proof that there exists a cosmic mental radio, which may well have connected the more highly developed peoples of countless worlds for many years.

Those who listen within in silence, having become completely quiet, may on occasion unexpectedly participate in such cosmic long-distance communications, although only for a few short moments.

X. *Cosmic Contacts*

For the time being, attempts are made to approach the possibility from the technical side. We will speak about it briefly.

Since the time scientists of the status of Albert *Einstein* have accepted cosmotelepathic contacts and information as technically attainable possibilities, they have been and are being investigated by the research institutes of large industrial firms, such as the Rand Corporation, the Bell Telephone Company, Westinghouse, General Electric and, above all, the research center of the U.S. Army in Redstone in behalf of the U.S. Government.

Science has recognized that such contacts will be of decisive importance to future astronautics because of the velocity beyond the speed of light of space-bridging cosmic exchange of thought.

In this connection, the U.S. neurologist Dr. A. Puharich has examined the various possibilities that may exist for specially trained astronauts to establish precise telepathic contacts among themselves and with the Earth.

He believes that properly trained personnel will, in the foreseeable future, also be able to influence and operate the control mechanisms of airplanes, rockets and spaceships by telepathic, rather telekinetic, means.

It is known that Soviet scientists are conducting research aimed at similar targets, that is, the achievement of remote transmission of thought impulses amplified by corresponding instruments. We assume, however, that for political reasons essential findings are being kept secret.

Since these experiments in space telepathy have not yet gone beyond the experimental stage and since telepathically gifted persons, "receivers" as much as "senders," are still relatively scarce, more highly developed beings of other worlds have so far found little opportunity to get in touch with earthmen.

Evidently, tests of this kind have been unsuccessful until now, including research conducted with sensitives. Messages transmitted by them are often so distorted that it is impossible to reconstruct the information actually received.

Meanwhile, the unfamiliarity of such mental remote transmissions may have triggered more fear, confusion and defense than understanding and receptiveness, just as a jungle monkey might be dumbfounded by a modern computer at work, probably reacting with fear and defensive gestures.

Passive psychic sensitivity, respectively mediumship, is an inadequate and hard-to-control means of contact, leading at best to pseudo-contacts with the contents of other people's subconscious.

Reliable cosmic contacts obviously require *active-dynamic mentally sensitive alertness* and a receptiveness free from all tension, as they have only rarely been attained up to the present.

Our positive possibilities of making such contacts will increase, however, to the extent that our understanding for different beings, life styles and mental worlds increases. So must our readiness to reach out and establish contact, and our still primitive earthbound ethics must expand into cosmic ethics, to reverence for all life in the universe as well as to the consciousness of our co-responsibility for the common advancement of all thinking beings in the universe.

Thus the first steps will be taken toward mutual interstellar understanding and information.

That possibility does exist and may be expected, because the creator of all life forms on the Earth as in other worlds of the universe is *Spirit*.

In experiments lasting millions of years, Spirit is systematically creating ever more suitable and perfect bodily instruments and opportunities for self-realization among the biocosmic conditions and ecological possibilities prevailing in the various worlds.

XI. *Keyword of the Aquarian Age*

The creator of all life forms on the Earth as in the universe, Spirit, is common to all life in the cosmos as its innermost nucleus.

All men, irrespective of physical differences, and all living creatures on this planet form a great life-unit when viewed bioenergetically. In the same manner, viewed cosmoenergetically, all creatures in the universe are vital force fields or spirit entities and internally *one,* irrespective of their myriad different forms, levels of unfoldment and maturity.

Moreover, they are aware, to different degrees, of the further fundamental fact that they are continuously connected and one with the "Cosmic Kybernetes," the Spirit of life whom men call "God."

In the last 5,000 years, that realization has only been granted in full to a few individuals who have awakened to the Inner Light and cosmic consciousness. In the Aquarian Age, it will gradually become common property.

Man will realize that he is a microcosm in which all

the substances, powers and possibilities of the macrocosm are present as seeds capable of developing.

And he will more and more achieve harmony between his inner world and the external universe.

The keyword of the Aquarian aeon is: *unity*.

Everything striving and leading toward that unity corresponds to the spirit of the Aquarian Age, such as endeavors for economic cooperation and political unification up to the United Nations; in addition, modern technical media of communication, such as radio and television; attempts at introducing a uniform global language, a brother tongue—aside from men's mother tongue; further, efforts for bringing religions and creeds together, for the overcoming of war and the creation of a united humanity living together in peace and liberty.

Despite all setbacks, evolution is steadily progressing toward the time when all men and peoples will grow together into a dynamic unity, out of which the spiritual unity of mankind will ultimately blossom.

If we look at it in this way, the Aquarian Age proves to be an epoch of universal friendship and reciprocal advancement.

This new spirit of unity, which throbs ever more strongly in mankind, is leading to the unchaining and unfolding of hitherto latent forces and specific talents in individuals and the collective development of power in mankind as a unit. These forces and abilities will enable men to establish contact and exchange information, with or without technical means, not only among themselves on the Earth but also with kindred spirits in other worlds.

Simultaneously, the realization of the inner unity of all thinking beings in the universe, among themselves and with the All-Spirit, which has until now been granted only to a few who have attained cosmic consciousness, will in future times become a general experience.

Looking further into the future, we see that earthly man will not only know that he is a microcosm but, beyond that, a microtheos. From then on he will put his surging divine-spiritual powers consciously into the service of cosmic evolution and the benefit of all sentient beings.

XII. *Cosmic Consciousness*

What filled Immanuel *Kant* with reverence and admiration, the starry skies above us, the moral law within us, will be recognized and affirmed by man of the Aquarian aeon as one and the same.

He will become vividly aware that the lawmaker within us is of the same nature as the cosmic lawmaker or "kybernetes" of the universal Godhead. We feel this "kybernetes" as our conscience, or inner voice, inner guidance, inner helper or innermost Self, depending on our level of development.

The universal Spirit is no longer the anthropomorphic (humanized) God of the Age of Pisces but the infinite, indwelling, creative and directive Spirit of Life whom we rightly also call the Spirit of Love.

Man of the Aquarian Age will become conscious of being an *indestructible spiritual vital force field* and simultaneously a "child of God."

In proportion to this realization, his life will become more permeated by Spirit and more filled with meaning.

He will have an intuitive knowledge of the universal plan and know about the oneness of the ground of the soul, the ground of the world and the ground of God, of which Meister Eckhart spoke already.

The life style of the New Man of the Aquarian aeon is both dynamic and cosmic. It is conditioned by the absolute certainty that everything is within and that within everything is *one,* that everything is forever recurring and progressing throughout eternity, rising to ever higher dimensions of consciousness, from the Earth to the universe, from the cosmic to the metacosmic, the Divine.

For everything is eternal, is Spirit and living manifestation of the ever self-realizing Godhead.

Thus man of the new era knows that the Spirit of Life is within him, around him and above him.

God works and realizes himself through him. He feels that he is a temple and vessel of cosmic powers and the creator of his world.

He knows the power of materialization of his thoughts, the power of transformation of his faith, the power of creation of his ideals as well as the eternal progressing of his spirit.

For him the inner and outer unity have merged with the universal unity.

These considerations are in no way a vision of the future and a utopia but reality even today.

For everything is contained in each of us as a seed. It depends upon ourselves how far the spirit of the New Age becomes alive and active in us, how far we learn to live from within, from the true center of our nature, by the spirit.

The more that takes place, the more we feel that we are the master of our life and destiny, as H. Kuenkel wrote in connection with the new era:

"Our entire life is tranformed from within. External events, experiences and destinies are no longer what they had been for us until now. They have lost their influence upon us. We recognize that they have never had that power of themselves, but that we ourselves bestowed that power upon them from the power treasure of our soul.

The world, as it appears to us, has a center of gravity in which it rests. That fixed center is our own heart.

The path of our destiny, no matter how tortuous it looked, is the straight way of the eternal life pouring through us into the world. We sense the inner law directing our destiny and know that we are one with it.

Man and his destiny are in truth one. No destiny can befall a man which does not have its exact counterpart in his soul.

Whoever has recognized himself, knows what to expect and what he needs, and he affirms it. He knows the harmony of the soul with destiny and the universe. And he changes his destiny by changing himself.

Because he knows that nothing alien can happen to him, he enjoys perfect calm.

Because he knows that his destiny arises from his own Self, he is perfect determination.

Deep calm and extreme determination are one in him—deepest thoughtfulness and affirmative activity.

From a passive sufferer he has become an active doer and shaper of his destiny.''

Small Intermezzo

EARTH'S BIPEDS

An item of information overheard by chance while fishing in the sea of mental waves. It originates with:
"Report 103 by Chief Life Researcher Sigma 83, Space Researchship Sir 9132":

"Report 10 on Sol 3—known by the Planetarians as "Earth"—and the prevailing life style of the oxygen-breathing bipeds is hereby supplemented as follows:

Repeated mental contacts confirm level of maturity 7 of the 60-degree evolutionary scale previously ascertained.

The number of the partly earthbound, partly water-bound, partly free-moving species should be increased by the 10th power over the figures of report 19.

The question remains how far their short life span impedes or favors their development.

Noteworthy contradiction: If the struggle for life is still normal behavior among the lower forms of life, it is not clear why the higher forms of the so-called "human beings" still remain at that level, why they fight each other individually and collectively up to planetary wars, instead of accelerating their evolution by uniting.

Development rate is nevertheless remarkable, considering the combination of mental assiduity and psychic instability and aggressiveness. Perhaps still requiring food, since they still subsist largely, like primitive creatures, by killing and incorporating subordinate life forms.

41

Energetic maintenance and transformation of physical form evidently still unknown.

Psychography shows growing mental tension resulting from deep-seated restlessness.

Emotiograms register chiefly red. Green as a sign of beginning spiritual unity and harmony recorded only in individual cases, recently more frequently, justifying a positive evaluation.

Still questionable whether, at the current transition from pre-atomic stage of civilization to cosmic era of evolution, self-destruction through abuse of nuclear energy because of spiritual immaturity can be avoided.

Positive indications are present, as culture meter shows high peaks in isolated instances against deep drops.

Amazing ignorance of fundamentals of life: mental and spiritual energies still underdeveloped in comparison with other abilities. Kinetic effects of deliberate aiming of thought and willpower have so far been achieved only by a few isolated earthmen.

Cosmic thinking recognizable only in rudimentary form. Correspondingly inadequate are the ideas of sensitive persons about our space research ships, called UFOS by them.

Result: for the time being, planetary unity and maturity corresponding to level 8 are still lacking, but a good start has been made.

Only a few individuals have so far reached cosmic maturity of level 10: considerable positive tendencies as well as the capacity for love, for sacrifice for spiritual goals and an unflinching perseverance in striving for self-realization and greater perfection.

Prerequisites exist for later admission to the galactic community of the united cosmic spiritual entities.

Attention! End of report. Instruments indicate listening in of a telepathically feebly endowed earthman."

THE MYSTERY OF LIFE

I. *Life—Older than the Stars*

One of the many unanswered questions concerns the *origin of life*. We are only today, at the beginning of the cosmic age, getting closer to understanding the answer.

The materialist view of life has been unmasked by nuclear physics as inadequate.

Matter is only another form of *energy,* just as ice is another crystallized congealed form of water. Matter is "frozen energy."

Ancient Hindu wisdom already took atoms to be energy vortexes behind which Spirit was the directing power. Energy and matter are two forms of manifestation of Spirit.

Seen from this *dynamic viewpoint,* the cosmos proves to be a spiritual universe according to its essential nature; according to its appearance, a world of order of actualized spiritual impulses or materialized thoughts directed by hierarchically organized spiritual powers.

From that vantage point, the *biblical story of creation* takes on a new look and new importance as an intuitive vision of Reality.

In the beginning there was God, the absolute All-Spirit, which is without a beginning, while his manifestation, the visible universe, has a beginning and an end.

Hindu wisdom speaks of the origin of the worlds as the exhalation or emanation of Brahma—the manifesting expanding universe—followed by the reverse current after billions of years.

Let us take a brief, quick-motion synoptical view of the first billion years after the outflowing of individual Spirit seeds and visible matter from the primordial matrix of the All-Spirit.

"God created heaven and earth." The All-Spirit manifested part of himself in a number of *spiritual entelechies,* individual force fields with the urge for self-realization and self-completion. Another part of himself was manifested as *energy* which condensed on a small scale into elementary particles, electrons, atoms, molecules—to "matter." On a large scale, it condensed into primordial nebulae out of which the galaxies with their billion solar systems and hot glowing planets formed.

On the originally "desolate and empty" planets "light and darkness," "land and water" separated from each other in the course of aeons, until the change of "day and night," due to the rotation of the planets, became visible.

The history of creation further teaches how, on the third day of creation, the All-Spirit assigned to his "children," the "entelechies" of individual vital energy fields, the task of utilizing the physical force fields of the atoms, of conquering the realm of matter and of embodying in it in various forms.

In molecular combination games lasting billions of years, they learned to transform inorganic matter into *organic matter* and to construct ever higher vital structures. In that way, they built for themselves ever more complex and suitable tools of self-expression and self-realization.

Three or four billion years ago, the entelechies sensing, playing and working steadily on our planet discovered the usefulness of the carbon atom for the structure of larger molecular chains and with them, serviceable bodily covers.

In that way, the first *unicellular* life arose in the primeval seas, out of which the increasingly more complicated organisms of higher life forms developed. They also conquered the land where "the Earth brought forth grass, herb yielding seed after its kind, and tree bearing fruit," and next to the Earth, the "greater light of the sun to rule the day" became a source of and inducement to life.

In a similar way, the first form of *animal life* up to the aquatic mammals of the primeval seas developed; then the innumerable *animal forms* on the mainland and and the flying creatures in the air up to the birds appeared; in each case in accordance with an inherent invisible development plan.

Man—God of the Earth

Far over a million years ago, *man* came forward as the terrestrial climax of that evolution. According to the story of creation, man is "like God," destined to rule over animals and the entire Earth. He is called to perfect himself to the point of becoming a conscious image of God and attaining conscious union with God.

With the appearance of man, the Spirit of Life completed his works on the seventh day of creation. He "rested on the seventh day and blessed it."

The "seventh day" *is still today*—and it is evidently man's task in turn to continue and complete the work of unfoldment. He should do so in the growing awareness that he is a child of God, entrusted with a planetary task, just as other beings in other worlds may have been given planetary tasks which will in time expand into cosmic missions.

The Realm of Life

It is therefore not true, as many believe, that life on our planet is a mere chance appearance, unique in the universe. Rather, Spirit-directed life is the purpose and goal of all cosmic evolution.

In reality, *life as an expression of Spirit is older than the stars,* and it will survive the aging and dying of stars just as that of each of its momentary physical forms thanks to its inherent creative powers.

At bottom, life forms are essentially *Spirit* in two ways: first, because their bodies are forms of manifestation of Spirit, and secondly, behind every organism there is the imperishable vital force field of an individual spirit supporting it. At heart, every living being senses that fact.

That is why *religion*—the consciousness of our inner connection with the Universal Spirit—is an original predisposition operating in man as a push forward and a pull upward. That is the reason why he is never content with the present but is forever striving to expand his sphere of life, activity and control and to become a clear-sighted transformer and shaper of his environment, instead of a part and object of it.

Thus he created *tools* for himself, serviceable mechanisms, starting with the invention of the *wheel* and the discovery of *fire.*

He used the force of fire for melting metals and fabricating metal alloys in a blowpipe stove, and he made bronze tools, weapons and ornaments.

This was followed by the discovery of *iron* and other minerals. About the same time, he invented *writing, from knot-writing and cuneiform to alphabet writing, as a means for nailing down and communicating information and knowledge.*

In turn, this started the development of the arts, the sciences and technology, followed by agriculture and husbandry.

Realizing that they were more likely to succeed through cooperation than by working alone, men decided to live together in villages and towns. They united in nations and finally formed continental and planetary communities aimed at realizing the ideal of a *United Mankind.*

In spite of all those achievements, the first minutes of the "Seventh day of creation" have hardly gone by. Ahead of man there lies an infinite period of terrestrial and cosmic evolution.

II. *Man's Task*

Among several hundred thousand species of plants and a good million species of animals on this planet, man has surfaced as the dominating life form. And he is obviously structured to grow even beyond himself, reaching ever higher spiritual and cosmic stages of unfoldment.

Physically, man is a child of the Earth; spiritually, heir to the universe and an infant of the infinite Spirit of Life.

According to his inner nature, he is older than the Earth, and the form of his body also shows that he has been on this planet much longer than he had suspected.

Dream memories of lepidodendrons and struggles with saurians, legends and myths of folklore about dragons and other antediluvean animals, together with other ancestral memories latent in the collective unconscious all point to that fact.

Already a million years ago and even earlier, when man "was still closer to his eternal origin" (Daqué), he evidently had a religion and culture to which today, however, no visible traces bear witness.

Since even the memory of them has been submerged, the question remains whether perhaps the legendary "paradise" of mankind was not on the Earth but on another planet, so that later, when there was no turning back, emigration from it felt like being exiled from the paradise of an older, more highly developed cultural world.

Today man realizes more than before that he is a creature of energetics, a vital force field, the center and "owner" of which is not the greedy and erring *ego* but the superconscious *Self* which does not only direct his conscious and subconscious but also the cell processes of his body.

Depending on its size, the body consists of 20-30 trillion cells, each cell in turn of trillions of molecules and every molecule of several hundred thousand atoms. We can well imagine, therefore, what a quintillionfold task the guiding Self has to accomplish unceasingly. Starting with the structure and growth of its bodily covers in each life, it repeats, condensed into weeks and months, a development which it took nature originally millions of years to achieve.

The physical, chemical and energetic structure and the life processes of the body are so complicated that they can only be supervised and directed by a super-mechanic cybernetic power.

Depending on how we look upon it, we call this guiding power in man the "inner physician," the "soul," the "inner guidance" or the "inner helper." Its operation is unmistakable even when the simplest healing of a wound is at stake, and more so in connection with every process of recovery. It demonstrates how sovereignly the Self as the "inner physician" controls and directs the giant realm of the viruses, genes, chromosomes, hormones, enzymes and ferments of the cells and cell unions, the organs, nerves, muscles and tissues, including the blood circulation and lymph stream.

This power of the Self is most clearly seen in *spiritual healings* which show that the Self is inwardly connected with the cosmic kybernetes, the All-Self or God, and how far it is able to draw from the divine reservoir of strength.

Modern Man—Only a Beginning

Today we know already a small part of the decisive laws governing the higher development of all life, its meaningfulness, and the fact that all that lives is permeated by Spirit. We are beginning to sense the silent operation of invisible regulative and formative forces in the organism, and the oneness and wholeness of creation where all living things determine their own destiny to a large extent.

Similarly, we are more or less aware that we humans, being the current end product of the evolution of earthly forms, do not stop in our development for one moment.

In a world of eternal change, where evolution and progress in all areas are taking place at a steadily increasing rate, we must learn to translate our knowledge into practical wisdom, so as to continue to master the perpetually changing life pattern.

Every day, we are standing at a new beginning—and we feel that we ourselves are the beginning.

Undreamed of new adventures await us. To the extent that our mental horizon and our material surroundings expand, the points of contact with the still uncharted and unconquered areas increase and with them, the multiplicity of the possibilities for development.

We are not only developing mentally and socially, but also physically in regard to the excellence and efficiency of our bodies.

If we wish to get a clear idea of this, however, we have to encompass millions of years with our remote vision.

From a cosmic viewpoint we realize that man is on the steep road from today's *homo sapiens* to the *homo superior* of the future—on a road that knows neither a stop nor a final goal but only an *infinite upward,* as far as our superconscious sensing can feel its way into the light-ocean of the future.

The history of humanity up to the present is but a cosmic moment in time. In that one moment man has soared from a condition of relative sleep and imperfection to the mastery of his fellow creatures and has begun to subject the Earth to his will. It is only himself he does not yet know and cannot control.

Control over the powers of the Earth, conquest of space and the immediate cosmic vicinity of the Earth are only a beginning of what man is able to accomplish.

If we equate the circle of human evolution with one day, mankind has hardly passed through more than the first minutes of its day of existence.

We have therefore not reached the climax of our evolution, let alone the end, as skeptics and pessimists believe, but we are standing at the *beginning of human history*.

We are living, in the words of a well-known astronomer, "in the wonderful freshness of the dawn of earthly life, and a day of almost unimaginable length with unthinkable possibilities of human development is still ahead of us

. . . .

. . . .When our remote descendents consider this long period of time from the other side, they will think of it as the foggy morning of world history. And men of our times will seem to them like shadowy, heroic figures who cleared their way through the jungle of ignorance, error and supersitition in order to track down truth, master the forces of nature, creating with their help a world where it is worth while living."

Let us see what kind of development possibilities our future holds for us when we look at it from the other side, with the eyes of homo superior.

III. *Man and Robot*

The cultural pessimist, Oswald *Spengler,* foresaw the decline not only of the Western world but of all humanity:

"Measured by the plant and animal worlds on this planet, the history of mankind is an abrupt decline and fall of a few millennia . . . . We men of the 20th century are going down with our eyes open . . . ."

He was supported by Karl *Jaspers* in *Die geistige Situation der Zeit* (1931; *Man in the Modern Age,* 1933). He expected the words of the poet to come true, "I foresee a time when God no longer takes pleasure in mankind and when he will again destroy everything in order to rebuild it in a rejuvenated creation."

Another writer, Ludwig *Klages,* in *Der Geist als Widersacher der Seele (Mind as the Antagonist of the Soul)* also feared the approaching end of humanity, "because the cross section of world history does not show any facts justifying hope, but many demanding the worst predictions."

These and other philosophers who prophesied the fate of Sodom and Gomorrah to mankind were lacking that keen insight which perceives the underlying primary trends—the push forward and the pull upward—behind the secondary surface confusion.

They overlooked the imperceptibly but steadily operating dynamic powers of regeneration which account for the fact that the path of mankind's destiny is no "abrupt decline and fall of a few millennia" but an eventful high-altitude path of progressive development to ever higher levels of future perfection.

Technology—Servant of Man

Spengler considered the increasing technicalization of life a main cause of the decline.

"The rate of inventions grows to fantastic proportions . . . . The number of hands required grows with the number of machines, because technical luxury increases every other kind of luxury and because this artificial life is becoming ever more artificial."

He believed that "nobody can change anything about this fate of machine technology which is now drawing to a close. Creation rises against the creator, machine against man . . . . It forces him along its own course . . . . The fallen victor is dragged to his death by the frenzied horses. Only dreamers believe in a way out. Optimism is cowardice . . . ."

Let us contrast this end-of-the-world panic of the pessimists with the facts:

We have seen that man began thousands of years ago to free his head and hands by creating *tools* to reduce his labor. One of the first was the mill-wheel driven by the water of a brook, which was soon followed by further mechanisms.

This development got a powerful upswing by the discovery of steam power, electric energy and the mineral wealth of fuel: steam engines, electric motors and other power engines helped him to improve his living conditions.

Today, man is building machines, servomechanisms, that work largely independently, are self-regulating and direct the machines and production of entire plants.

He is aiming at *fully automatic robots* with equipment copied from the working methods of the human brain, and the capacity to build new and better robots in turn.

Man or Robot?

With modern peak creations the *new age of electronics and cybernetics has been ushered in,* since the new type of machine or robot does not only reduce *mechanical* work but deprives man of more and more of his controlling *mental work.*

Robots of the future will no longer be mechanisms but "energisms," while man is a "spiritual *dynamism"* according to his nature.

As "energisms," robots not only process data, but in so doing they *learn*. They produce new data, and in this way take over additional functions of the human brain.

In a certain sense they possess *"consciousness,"* something that goes beyond "matter" and "energy," even if they will never develop *self-consciousness* like man.

Even today robots surpass man in speed, accuracy, reliability and tirelessness as far as the ability to think logically, to draw conclusions and make decisions is concerned. They are able to receive speechlike impulses or data, to memory store, compare and process them, to modify their instructions, and much more.

But one thing they cannot do: they are unable to think about themselves, *to think and act creatively* like man.

If we should find "robot psychologists" on this planet in a hundred years or so, it will not be a kind of new psychiatrist but logicians able to detect and correct error switchings and disturbances in the electronic or "positronic" robot brains.

Being the work of man, even the most developed robot is unable to replace, let alone surpass, either the human mind or the brain. The human brain is and remains the most perfect automatic electrochemical device for the processing of information, surpassing the performance of all computers and robots in today's world a thousand times. The same is true for the future, because of the steady further development of the brain.

Among other reasons, this is so because each single one of the 12 billion gray brain cells is a much more complicated structure than a computer, and because every gray cell is so cleverly connected with the others by innumerable automatic links (synapses) that man's performance level is thereby multiplied in geometrical progression.

This is *one* of the many facts that substantiate and clarify the realist optimism of those who assert that an infinite future lies ahead for mankind and that in ages to come the slogan will not be "man *or* robot" but "man *and* robot!"

It is always up to man himself what *he* will make of technology and robot servants.

And if in a thousand years the social, economic and political processes and problems of a united mankind are perhaps controlled by a central giant brain for the benefit of all, the human factor will neither then nor later be eliminated, but always hold a key position.

Before that development, however, man will have taken another step in the control of natural forces and succeed, not only as today in nuclear fission and fusion, in transforming *matter into energy,* but also in transmuting *energy into matter.* This he will do first indirectly by means of special equipment and finally directly through mental impulses, through tele-energetic (by remote action) psychoelectronic impulses of thought or volition.

IV. *Man's Future*

"If the spirit had no presentiment of the future and if it had to enclose all its thoughts within the limits of its small living space, it would never take so much trouble, never risk the struggle for life and death so often."

These words by *Cicero* are confirmed by today's psychodynamic view of the world. Everywhere in nature and in life we can observe an endeavor to make provision for the future, pointing to the seeds of things to come that are embedded in all life.

Especially in man do we notice various signs of systematic provision for *man of the future.* Like *Teilhard de Chardin,* the natural scientist K.C. *Schneider* sees "the divine Spirit directly at work in the living world, in the sense that it is becoming more and more like God in the course of the development of ever higher beings."

Let us look at the unfolding of earthly life as a cosmic film where every picture covers a thousand years and let us see what is being shown in this quick-motion survey in meditative reflection upon ourselves and the universe.

If we consider that the speed of the individual stages of development and progress increases in geometric proportion, we get an inkling of the infinite wealth of technical and spiritual know-how awaiting our future descendents.

We then realize with *Herder* that *in each of our powers infinite development possibilities* lie hidden, which have not yet been activated so far but will be unfolded in all directions in the coming aeons.

Seeds of Things to Come

Man of genius, until now an exception, will in a distant future be a normal occurrence. As a psychodynamicist, this *"homo superior"* has unfolded the seeds of development and latent talents contained in homo sapiens to an unimaginable degree.

In this fragmentary preview we can only describe a few details.

What is most noticeable in man of the future is his greater *sensory wealth*. Along with the specialized senses of sight, hearing, touch, smell and taste, with their far greater range of perception, new senses have unfolded which are only latent or rudimentary in present-day man. They open new ways of perception and new dimensions of reality to homo superior.

Together with his refined senses for time, direction and danger, which surpass the sense of direction and scent of animals, it is the sense of optimum "rightness," coupled with an exceedingly sensitive flair for inspiration from the unconscious and intuition from the superconscious, that distinguishes him.

Even more remarkable is a kind of *X-ray sense* that

he possesses: his alertness for influences from energy fields, for other people's sympathetic or antipathetic thoughts, feelings and tendencies. To this we may add his ability for remote communication which is further reinforced by relevant instruments.

We men and women of the twentieth century are proud of our ability to think logically; but compared with us, homo superior is a "power-thinker" able to set persons and things in motion through pointed dynamic impulses of thought and volition.

The three-dimensional world of our environment has expanded for him into a four-dimensional world of truth.

Manifestations of "parapsychic" forces, which are today taken seriously by only a few specialists, are for him part of his conscious activity.

He is not only master of the supramental abilities of telepathy and telekinesis, but can also trigger sympathetic tele-energetic changes in the intentions and actions of others.

Moreover, he is in *telemental contact* with his cosmic surroundings. This achievement not only enables him to exchange information with alien beings but to unite with them for the purpose of physico-mental remote operations.

Corresponding to the amplitude of his mental powers and abilities is the affluence of his life in the centralized world State of a united mankind with a common language —a world in which the goals of the UN Charter have largely been reached.

We see homo superior normally active in a variety of complex fields. He always knows how to coordinate mentally and solve his problems in that *spirit of unity and friendship* which is characteristic for his world.

In so doing, he has at his disposal an immense number of self-acting servomechanisms and superrobots which respond to specific thought impulses.

What is remarkable, in addition, is that science and

religion, art and life are a living *unity*. Religion to him is not a mere believing-it-to-be-true but knowledge and wisdom.

He knows that his spiritual core, the "inner kybernetes," his *Self,* is indissolubly connected with the All-Self.

The Spirit of love and life is not an object of faith for him but a matter of experience. He is aware of the oneness of his vital energy field with the cosmic primordial force field of the All-Spirit.

What is today the supreme goal of human endeavor, "cosmic consciousness" and "harmony with the infinite," is for him the natural basis of his life.

Viewed thus, he must look to us like a demigod, although he himself is conscious of having passed through but a few of the first stages of an infinite process of development.

Humboldt already realized that "every natural law that reveals itself to us allows us to infer a higher, still unrecognized one; for nature is eternal growth, always engaged in forming and unfolding." And so is man.

The universe is no mechanically running clockwork, let alone a chaos, but a *dynamic cosmos:* a carefully planned, orderly system, a Spirit-permeated, hierarchically structured, harmonious whole, behind whose manifoldness there lies an ultimate oneness.

Having faith in this unity means remaining calm in the ups and downs of life and sure that the powers for goodness and perfection at work in the world will always gain the upper hand.

What *Fichte* called "the destination of the scholar" is the life task of each one of us. When we look at the future and the infinite viability within us, we should "be happy about the vision of the vast field we have to cultivate, happy that we feel up to the task and that *our task is infinite.*"

WE CHILDREN OF THE UNIVERSE

I. *Microcosm and Macrocosm*

"Philosophy does not find anything in the entire cosmos that it does not also find in man. For the hand of Him Who created heaven and earth has also created the microcosm. That is why the external heaven is a signpost for us to the inner, and the inner, a gate to the universe."

Paracelsus

The most recent findings of space exploration have revealed a picture of the universe which agrees remarkably with the almost forgotten conceptions of past ages and the cosmic visions of the great seers of former civilizations. In many statements of modern astronomers and cosmophysicists we hear the ancient wisdom of a *spiritual bond* which unites the multiplicity of terrestrial and cosmic appearances in a universal order, causing us to sense one and the same All-Spirit behind all happenings.

Self-Reflection—All-Reflection

Actually, there is not only the *external,* technical way of astronomy to make us aware of the All-harmony, but also the more progressive *inner* way of self-reflection, which reveals the mystery of the universe more perfectly.

We have learned that the astromants of Atlantis and Ancient India "felt the nature of the stellar realms directly when they were in a state of clairvoyance." This explains the wisdom of astrosophy and cosmology. Like the priest-visionaries of the ancient peoples, in whose legends about the heavens and cosmic symbolism there is more wisdom than meets the eye, the present generation should and can learn the *approach to the wonders of the universe from within.*

We are microbelike, infinitesimal dwellers on the third planet of a relatively small sun in the 100 billion solar systems of our galaxy, the Milky Way. Even the fact that we are able to apprehend the nature and shape of the universe by means of instruments created by us, that we can deduct from the light of the stars and nebulae their inner structure and realize our own position in the universe proves that the Universal Soul itself dwells within us, *that we are children of the universe.*

We become sure of this when we delve ever deeper within ourselves in meditative self-reflection, until it reaches the stage of All-reflection and we become aware of both our total security and the spiritual relationship and unity of all beings in the cosmos.

The great minds of mankind have since time immemorial sensed or recognized this fact, as the historian J. *Bachofen* (1815-1887) explained, "It was the all-dominating view of Antiquity that terrestrial and celestial matters obey identical laws and that a great harmony pervades the transient and the eternal worlds. Earthly development will strive until it fully reaches and realizes the cosmic example of the stellar bodies.''

This development will reach its first high noon in the Aquarian Age.

In self-reflection and All-reflection earthbound human thinking expands to *cosmic thinking,* to that All-understanding that reaches farther than telescopes and radar. Through it we experience the awakening of a condition called *"spiritual vision"* by Rudolf *Steiner,* which grasps the nature of the world and the Spirit of the Whole beyond the forms of appearance. Through it we become aware that the *heart of the universe is throbbing within us* and that life in all areas of the cosmos and within us is the *same one life.*

The Cosmosophic Standpoint

In meditative All-reflection we pass from the usual cosmic *analysis,* as is done by astronomy and astrophysics, to *cosmosynthesis:* the vision of the total unity of the world process. In so doing, we touch upon the meaning of the whole and the spiritual unity behind the diversity of appearances. Beyond the previous and current theories of the structure of the universe we reach the true *theoria* in the sense of Plotinus: the *vision* and realization of Reality, as far as it can be understood by the human mind at its present level of maturity.

Cosmosophy (All-wisdom as the fruit of All-reflection) recognizes in the universe a living, hierarchically structured whole where every part—every stellar body and every creature—is in dynamic reciprocity with the cosmic kybernetes or directing Spirit of Life as well as every other part and every sentient being. In both the astrology and the cosmology of the Ancients, fragments of this knowledge of prehistoric man, who was still more intimately connected with the Spirit of the Whole, have been preserved.

The historian and statesman Christian K.J. *von Bun-*

sen (1791-1860) rightly spoke in this connection of the "innate feeling of the relationship of man as the microcosm, the divine world in miniature, to the macrocosm, the divine world on a large scale. The natural and spiritual cosmos realize the same idea, the former in space, the latter in time . . . .

. . . As an eternal thought is inherent in the Earth and all the stars, which directs them and makes of them part of an organic whole, there dwells in man a *presentiment* of his relationship to mankind, and of mankind's relationships as a unity to the universe and its first cause. Man becomes conscious of the *God within him* as the Spirit of the Good. His conscience is a knowledge about that eternal love and reason which men should realize in the course of their development. Mankind is not only the poem that the Godhead has written in its eternal thoughts and unfolded in time, it is also the poet of this unfoldment of the divine idea in space."

Thus, the development of mankind points to the cosmic space beyond the terrestrial.

As Above—So Below

Sooner or later, Self-reflection and All-reflection lead us to that age-old wisdom expressed over 4,000 years ago by *Thoth Hermes:*

"It is true, no lie, certain, and to be depended upon, the superior agrees with the inferior, and the inferior with the superior, to effect that one truly wonderful work. As all things owe their existence to the will of the only One, so all things owe their origin to the One only thing, the most hidden, by the arrangement of the Only God. That One Only thing is the father of all things in the universe. Its power is perfect, after it has been united to a spirituous earth."*

---

*Translation from Dr. Sigismund Bacstrom's Collection of Alchemical Manuscripts, (18th century) *Tabula Smaragdina.*

In other words: the scale of the infinitely big has its correspondence in the infinitely small. One who has the eyes to see perceives in a grain of sand at the beach a universe of myriads of atomic solar systems—a miniature of the cosmos, in which the Spirit of the Whole is as present and at work as in the galaxies.

All wonders of the macrocosm have their equivalent in the human being. In him the radii of time and eternity, of the finite and infinite, cross. Man and the universe are *one* like an original image and its likeness. Wherever we look, there is heaven: within us, as above us. All we have to do is open our inner eyes to perceive the Light of the Eternal within and above us behind the smoke screens of this transient world: the God within us and the Godhead of the universe.

Seen microphysically, our body is a host of billions of universes in motion. As we close our fist, microcosmic world systems that lie unimaginably far apart approach each other, thanks to a will that is incomprehensible to them. It may well take millions of years till the mini-universes that form one cell of the fingertip and those belonging to a cell of the palm are noticed by each other.

We walk across the Earth without thinking—and we have no idea that we are gliding over microcosmic star islands, over quintillions of microworlds full of life . . . A thinking resident of one of these worlds of the microcosm may perhaps admire the unimaginable size of his universe . . . . And how large is it in reality? Seen with human eyes, tinier than a grain of sand . . . .

Similarly, our own universe may well be a dust particle of a living cell in a metacosmic superworld.

When we human beings have recognized the *spiritual unity of mankind* in the Aquarian Age, when we have attained to *planetary maturity* and have become candidates for *cosmic maturity,* we shall get a clearer idea of these relationships. Then we shall advance from the status of earthmen to that of universal citizens, becoming some day that to which we are called: participants in God's omnipotence and creative collaborators of the God-head.

II. *"In my Father's House are Many Mansions"*

In his farewell talks, Jesus spoke the words, "In my Father's house are many mansions." This important statement points first to the multidimensionality of the world and the diversity of the higher spiritual realms which are inhabited and traveled through by the beings of all worlds to the degree of their cosmic maturity.

In addition, these words may be taken as a reference to the infinite number of cosmic worlds whose life forms are externally unlike those of the Earth's, but are inwardly related, because the same one Spirit unfolds and realizes itself in all.

Finally, these words are a reminder for us to remember that those beings who incarnate in the earthly school of life may earlier have lived and learned in many other worlds in other physical forms, and that they will incarnate again on a thousand more cosmic worlds in the course of their future world migrations.

Like every creature in the universe, man is a child of God. In the divine universe there are "many mansions," countless worlds where there is life, and on each, myriads of life forms exist. Life is not only a terrestrial but a cosmic phenomenon.

Our Earth, with its wealth of creatures and forms, offers life only *one* among billions of possibilities for existence and completion. It encompasses only an infinitesimal secton of the cosmic realm of life with its quintillion communities of living beings.

In meditation we understand Goethe's words, how much "everything perishable is but an analogy" and how the laws applicable to the three-dimensional sense world accessible to us have their correspondence on millions of other higher-dimensional mental and spiritual worlds—and we have not even the faintest idea to what extent those worlds are brimming with life!

Wisdom of the Astromants

The astromants of remote antiquity knew how difficult it is to communicate one's insights to persons who are spiritually unawakened. That is why they spoke in symbols which show a remarkable resemblance to the symbolic language of the unconscious. To understand it, the *universal sense of the soul* has to be activated.

They knew, as Count *Keyserling* wrote, "that the free-willing and free-working human being is simultaneously an expression of cosmic willing and becoming." In him and with him the Spirit of the universe manifests and realizes itself.

With the astromants anthroposophy and cosmosophy were one: Knowledge about man was the microcosmic correspondence of their stellar wisdom. They saw in man the directing Spirit, creating for itself a bodily tool and field of activity suitable to its level of development, so as to realize its potential more completely from life to life and from star to star.

If they saw in the stars dwellings of angels and gods, it was partly a result of their universal vision, and partly their mental and/or physical contacts with cosmonauts of distant worlds—cosmic technical assistance experts—whose knowledge and abilities made them look like gods in comparison with human beings.

Here we have an explanation for the ever surging reference to the permeation of the universe by a soul, as *Democritus* (460-370 B.C.) taught. According to him, life on other stars is the rule, while worlds without life forms are the exception. Many great minds of Antiquity agreed with him.

Based on his inner vision, the Church Father *Origines*

(185-243) stated most clearly that the Earth is only one of untold worlds in the universe which are inhabited by thinking beings. He confirmed the age-old belief that the soul reincarnates after death upon the Earth or other more perfect worlds. He said that *the eternal life of the soul consists precisely in this wandering from world to world,* in the course of which it soars to ever higher heavenly worlds and brighter living conditions. He asserted that *our true home was not the Earth but the universe.*

Origines saw man rise to ever higher stages of spiritualization and godlikeness upon an infinite scale, until at-one-ness with the Spirit of Life and the worlds was finally attained.

Among those who became conscious of the infinite number of inhabited worlds we find, among many other mystics and cosmosophers, *Plotinus* (205-270). He became convinced of this fact when he attained cosmic consciousness. Simultaneously, he realized that many men reincarnate after death in more advanced worlds for further development according to the law of sowing and reaping (karma). The kind of world in which they reincarnate depends on the law of elective affinity.

Plotinus was granted a third intuitive insight when he recognized that the inhabitants of progressive worlds are in constant mental communication and communion. Earthmen, however, are seldom aware of it, because "one cannot comprehend the wonders of the universe with the mind but solely with the divine intellect, by turning inward—there where one becomes directly conscious of the living universe, that is, in that cosmic consciousness where our being is free from the limitations of normal consciousness. It is an elevation of the spirit in which we are transposed beyond the barriers of time and bodily existence into the omnipresence of the One—into the oneness with the One."

Infinity of the Worlds

What Plotinus and others who were filled with the

Inner Light of cosmic consciousness realized is that *we humans are not the only thinking beings,* that life forms exist in myriads of worlds which are externally similar to us, though more frequently dissimilar, but inwardly kindred. Through them Spirit works and realizes itself in the same way as through us. They and we are *equally children of the universe.*

Paracelsus (1494-1541) rightly considered it nonsense to believe that the Earth is the only stellar body inhabited by thinking beings and that we humans are a unique occurrence in the universe. The Scandinavian seer, *Immanuel Swedenborg* (1688-1772), too, became aware in his visions and auditions of the multiplicity of inhabited worlds and the manifoldness of alien life forms. He realized that all worlds and beings together form a *spiritual whole*—so to speak, individual cells in the organism of a macrocosmic universal man in whose development they share and collaborate.

Immanuel Kant (1724-1804) was another who dealt with the question of the nature and mentality of the inhabitants of the various space worlds.

In him, too, the cosmic yearning was alive, "Who knows, are those satellites not circling Jupiter so as to shine for *us* some day?" Like Origines he found comfort in the thought that the human soul can develop further in higher celestial worlds and that one day, like Diotima in Hölderlin's *Hyperion* "we shall migrate like swallows from one spring to another, through the large region of the sun and beyond to the golden shores of Sirius and the ghost valleys of Arcturus."

Lessing (1729-1781) also inferred from the belief in reincarnation that the human soul embodies itself again on more advanced worlds according to the degree of maturity it reached on earth, while other beings break away from lower worlds to incarnate on our planet.

He was seconded by *Herder* (1744-1803) in his talks

on transmigration. He saw in all planets residences for creatures of different kinds and forms.

In his words, the peoples of all the worlds in the cosmos form "a *universal choir* "which praises the Creator in different sounds and proportions but in the harmony of *one* power."

Goethe, too, expressed this conviction, *"if man is the first conversation that the nature of our planet holds with God, this conversation may be held on other planets at a much higher, deeper and comprehensive level."*

III. *Life in the Cosmos*

Compared with a day of life on earth, terrestrial humanity is only a few minutes old. It does not yet know what the sunrise of its earthly day of life will bring, what will be the morning of superman, the high noon of spiritual and universal man and the evening of the Godman fading away in the course of millions of years.

But even today a feeling is arising in man that the Earth is only his temporary home, while the universe is his eternal home. His task on earth is called self-realization; his cosmic task, God-realization. In the course of his wanderings through the worlds he should "become perfect, as his heavenly Father is perfect." (Matt. 5:48).

The Earth is mankind's nurse; its mother, the cosmos; its father, the infinite Spirit of Life. Man's body is born of the Earth and subject to decay like everything material; his innermost Self, however, is born of the universe and older than the stars.

What matters is that we should again become conscious of our inner eternity, our cosmic origin and future and our unity with the universe. The God within us knows that we come from beyond the stellar worlds, from a higher realm: the primordial being of the universal Godhead.

We World Travelers

We are world travelers who know that it is the same stars that lit the earthly nights when the first life rose from the primeval seas, when the first plants took root in the earth, when the sea creatures risked coming on land and when man finally began his triumphal march. Since then he has in endless incarnations again and again looked up at the same stars in the vague feeling of a kinship which goes deeper than the one linking him to the Earth.

On the same stars at which he gazed, other beings have created for themselves physico-organic, gaseous, plasmatic or other body covers and adapted to the prevailing ecological conditions.

But they all have one thing in common with the creatures of the Earth. Their material forms are subject to decay, while their souls follow the universal law of recurrence, advancing from lower to more and more highly developed worlds.

All of them are world travelers, like we humans, children of the universe who, originating in divine regions, descended into the physical universe through spritiual and mental realms. From here they return again to God, from life to life and from star to star. In a myriad forms of existence they learn to become more and more experienced and mature, approaching self-realization step by step—always on the way to themselves and to the universal Self.

For one who knows this, death has lost its sting. Even in this world and in spite of the perishableness of his physical cover, he is consciously living in the Eternal. He knows that he has always been there and will always exist and that each death is but a longer sleep and a fleeting moment of his eternal life.

As Inside—So Outside

As there are persons on earth who live in the antlike

delusion that the Earth is the only inhabited body in space and human beings are the "only elect of God," there are also beings in other worlds whose self-overestimation is proportionate to the limitation of their intellectual capacity and who consider themselves the only thinking beings in the universe.

But finally this childhood stage is overcome and those beings understand that their home is a star among stars. Their cosmic horizon expands sooner or later through the development of space travel, through contact with creatures of other constellations and, above all, through the mental contacts with more developed beings of other worlds and the realization of the omnipresence of life in the cosmos.

Thus, Giordano *Bruno* (1548-1600) envisioned the universe as filled with innumerable planetary dwelling-places of thinking beings. "God has created no empty houses, no uninhabited worlds in the universe, but has provided suitable tenants for each when the time has come." In fact, *life is as omnipresent as the Godhead.* Every creature in the universe is a carrier and instrument, workshop and field of activity of the world Spirit and indissolubly one with it.

Whether we turn inward or outward toward the universe, ultimately we attain the same realization of the All-unity of life. The old Hermetic word "As above, so below" is equallly valid for the higher dimension, *"As within, so without!"*

As the small corresponds to the big, the inner corresponds to the outer. In the cosmic order everything is simultaneously inner and outer, the visible external world being a shadow image of the invisible inner world, as Thoth Hermes announced. In modern parlance,

"Listen within yourselves—and you perceive the infinity of space and time—within yourselves and without. Out of the innermost of your being you hear the song of the stars, the harmony of the spheres. Because the human spirit is of the nature of God—not different from him but one with him as light is one with the sun.

On the outside everyone appears to be separated from everyone else, alone and left to himself. Within, he is a part and manifestation of the whole, connected and one one with all life in the universe.

Whoever has become aware of his divine Inner-All, knows that he is one with the "All."

The "All" within ourselves is not smaller than the cosmos. Yes, in the inner vision the spiritual universe in the depths of our nature appears to expand farther and farther—farther than the infinite stellar seas of the cosmos.

Within ourselves we find the radiant primordial center of all beings and all worlds. Because within us, there is the Spirit of Life. Self and Universal Self are one. In the supreme hour of our existence we all attain to the thrilling certainty expressed by a mystic, J.F. *Finck,*

"Inside and outside have merged in one heaven. The finite and the infinite have become one. I am intoxicated by the vision of the All. In my heart the heart of eternity is beating. My heart is the heart and dwelling-place of God, and the All-heart of the Godhead is my heart and my home."

The Universal Sense

In the depth of every soul the universal sense is slumbering. With its awakening, man becomes aware of his harmony with the infinite and the voices that resound incessantly through the universe, as well as of the currents, vibrations and messages flowing through the cosmos.

Nowadays, attempts are made to establish contact with thinking beings of other worlds by technical instead of inner means. *"Project OZMA"* was one of the first attempts to open a channel of communication with the nearest solar worlds through radio signals.

The scientists engaged in this project proceeded from the assumption that "aside from the known natural laws, there are evidently intelligent beings who share in influencing events in the universe and that, therefore, it would be important and should be possible to make contact with them."

Until today, the stars *Epsilon Eridani* and *Tau Ceti* (eleven light-years from the Earth), that is, their possible inhabitants, have not answered those radio communications. We should not draw hasty conclusions, however, since there may be many reasons for their silence and since such signals must be continued over longer periods of time and directed to numerous stars if success is to be achieved in this way.

In comparison with those external attempts at establishing contact, the inner way of mentally contacting other planets promises to be more successful, as the previous and further considerations explain.

IV. *Cosmo-Contacts*

For a self-realized man or woman the question does not arise whether the radiant jewels in the sky contain infinite life, often spiritually more advanced and perfect than that on the relatively young Earth, and whether they possess powers, abilities and knowledge of which we humans have no idea and can at best only get a faint notion in momentary mental contacts.

Thus I remember a series of dreams I had in my early childhood, when I had extremely varied visions of primeval worlds with saurianlike creatures, lepidodendrons and other Paleolithic trees, as well as of advanced worlds with glass-towered cities and luminous beings floating through the air. They filled me with a presentiment of a multiplicity of inhabited worlds and simultaneously with the realization that we go wrong by picturing creatures of other worlds as all too human.

Even if the elementary structure of all cosmic worlds resembles that of our home sun and earth, the prevailing physical, energetic, biological and ecological conditions differ on every stellar body, and the physical forms of their inhabitants are adapted to them.

On billions of worlds, life may well take billions of different forms, manifesting the superiority of mind over matter in ever different ways.

The same applies to the technical, ethical and spiritual evolution of the tenants of other worlds, a good reason why the question of *messages from other worlds* appears meaningless at first sight.

Of what use are signals from the universe which we cannot even perceive, because they are sent over still unknown physical, mental or spiritual wavelengths or sub-wavelengths? How can we ascertain that more developed creatures with cosmic senses follow events on our Earth, but consider it premature to contact us?

Let us remember that there are not only worlds for whose undeveloped dwellers we humans would look like gods, but far more others whose leading entities are both so far ahead of us and so differently developed that they do not think it worhwhile to open a channel to us.

Perhaps we should even be grateful that a cosmic power has kept us until now from getting in touch with totally alien mentalities of remote constellations, which might have led to the destruction of life on earth by ethically differently motivated and technically far superior beings.

Interstellar Communication

The problem of interstellar communication is more complex and complicated than we suspect. The difficulties may not only lie in the different types of evolutionary levels and mentalities but also in different measures of space and time. Time is a relative concept. How, for instance, are we to communicate with beings for whose consciousness a thousand planetary rotations correspond to one Earth hour, or whose day is equal to one Earth year?

Should this time dimension in which we move change, the face of the world would be totally different. This is why our world may appear to beings of another time dimension like a dream fantasy and, vice versa, their world to us.

In a corresponding *dilatation of time* the apparent solid matter of our bodies would dissolve in a loose cloud of whirling atomic solid matter and stellar clusters. Conversely, in a corresponding *contraction of time* millennia would be shortened to seconds; the becoming and dying of creatures, the growth of trees and houses, the change of things, would become imperceptible for us. Instead, we would see the breathing of the Earth encircled by the fiery hoop of the sun, we would perceive how the continents drift and change, and how the stars in heaven move among each other.

With increased quick motion the rotation of the stars would be so much accelerated that we would notice their motions as little as those of the atoms—and instead of a largely empty stellar space, we would be face to face with the compact matter of a metacosmic universe.

The cosmos contains a great deal that belongs to other dimensions of space, time and consciousness and is therefore imperceptible for us. On the other hand, many things that appear incomprehensible in our life and destiny may well be due to an influence from other dimensions.

Perhaps it is a good thing that the various bodies in space are so far apart in spite of our spiritual unity and the possibility of empathic cosmo-contacts!

Once their inhabitants have attained *cosmic maturity,* possibilities for bridging the spatial distances by technical, mental or spiritual means will be revealed to them.

In *Teilhard de Chardin's* words, we human beings have in any case passed only partially through the levels of *biogenesis* and *psychogenesis,* having only just begun with the real spiritual development, *noogenesis.* Only after the *noosphere,* the spiritual atmosphere of our planet, has reached a higher degree of efficiency radiating into cosmic space, will man achieve corresponding cosmo-contacts.

Then we shall see whether the descendants of those spacemen who visited our yet underdeveloped planet 100,000 years ago, consider the spiritual maturity of mankind adequate for admission to the galactic macrorealm and, after a successful adaptation to cosmic ways of thinking, to a hook-up with the intergalactic communication network.

There is a possibility that this may already take place in the Aquarian Age. Ultimately, it depends on *us* if and when the united mankind as a whole turns to its cosmic task in peace and freedom.

As the astronomer Harlow *Shapley* emphasized, in agreement with other biocosmologists, it is doubtless something wonderful to share in the greater life in the universe and to learn that we are related and united in a common cycle of being and development with brothers and sisters on remote planets as well as with our terrestrial friends, the animals and plants.

Teilhard de Chardin, too, wrote of the reciprocal enrichment which contact with more highly developed civilizations of other worlds would entail. As remote as it may still be, he believed that it would influence both sides positively in spiritual and philosophical, scientific and technical, ethical and religious matters.

But for the time being, we have as yet no part in the cosmic communication network, because we do not yet perceive the supramental uniform "inter-language" of the spirit, which connects countless worlds through empathy.

Cosmic Technical Assistance Experts

It was probably for the same reason that former space visitors were not recognized as such. Many myths and legends of ancient cultures concerning spirits and demons, luminous beings floating through the sky in fiery chariots, winged angels and floating gods give rise to the conjecture that *astronauts from foreign solar systems* may have lived among men at certain times.

Many of them may have possessed or assumed human form. Others evidently had a totally different form, such as the vague descriptions of winged beings that appeard to the prophet Ezekiel in a cloud of fire. The Bible contains many such descriptions.

Or we may remember the age-old chronicle, taken from the temple archives, of the Babylonian historian *Berossus,* a contemporary of Alexander the Great (356-323 B.C.). It begins with the creation and deluge and tells among other things about a dolphinlike being called *Oannes,* who is described as rising out of the sea by daytime and who understood human language,

"The being taught men writing, the arts and the various sciences. He taught them to build houses and draft laws. He instructed them in agriculture, handicrafts and everything that could help to humanize men and refine their customs."

If we diregard all non-essentials, we are led to think that a spaceman from a distant watery world visited the Earth, remaining in the sea by night and working among men as a cosmic development agent during the day. (It is well known that dolphins are among the most developed sea mammals, whose brain is no less complicated and richly structured than that of man.)

It would be exciting to examine the astral religions of the Ancient Indians, Persians, Babylonians, Chaldeans, Egyptians, Mayans, etc., with their myths about other inhabited worlds in regard to traces of cosmic development impulses to the still undeveloped vital realms in all possible worlds. The frequent promises of such beings to return later for renewed assistance may also point to that fact.

We do not know how many inventions, how much ethical and spiritual progress are due to the educational influences of cosmic observers and development agents, how much knowledge flows from extraterrestrial sources to us.

Since the population of the Earth has today the possibility to tear itself to pieces and destroy itself through modern weapons, it could be that galactic guardians think the time has come to send new missions of cosmic helpers to our planet to further peace and progress.

V. *All-harmony*

For the time being, only a few individuals among us will soar physically into cosmic space. Mentally, however, *each of us* can share in the ascension to the stars, because the spirit within us is a child of the universe, not subject to the limitations of space and time and the field of gravity of the Earth. He can experience his oneness with the All-life.

Already on the level of the collective unconscious and more so in the area of the superconscious is man not only interconnected with man, soul with soul, like the cells in the body organism, but being with being, life with the life in all the worlds of the cosmos.

Even today, those who listen within feel for seconds that they are touched and accosted by other regions of life, remote space worlds. Even today, voices from the All, the universe, resound sometimes, telling us of cosmic realms.

If we delve still deeper, we reach the region of the All-conscious and God-consciousness, from which we draw intuition, mental messages from remote cultures, whose wisdom and power may be millions of years ahead of our own.

As our physical body is in touch with universal energy fields through the energy fields of the stars, through myriads of light rays, mental and spiritual impulses, and is influenced thereby, our stellar body, the soul, is intimately connected with the Spirit of the universe and the vital realms of other worlds.

It is from there that we become certain that we are *children of the universe,* Light-thoughts of the Spirit of Life and Light. We hear the music of the spheres of the *harmonia mundi,* the world harmony of which *Kepler* spoke, we feel the reciprocal influence of all living things in the universe and the drive toward higher development inherent in all life.

One Life—One Spirit

Giordano *Bruno* (1548-1600) was burnt at the stake after seven years' imprisonment, because he spoke of the infinity of the universe which he considered permeated by a divine soul. He was convinced that there are countless life forms advancing from incarnation to incarnation, from lower to higher worlds, and that together they form a single living All-organism permeated by the Spirit of the Godhead.

As varied as are the evolutionary ways of life in the countless worlds of the cosmos, in the end they converge, merging in the course of progressive spiritualization and manifesting the unity of all life. *All development in the universe aims at the growing domination of the Spirit, and the individual life forms are his workshops.*

Whether one being lives on the Earth, another on a planet of Andromeda, a third in the microworld of an atom—each touches the depths of the universe in the depth of his nature. In each the Spirit of Life breathes. The ground of the soul, the ground of the world, and the ground of God are *one* ground, as Meister Eckhart had recognized.

Cosmosophy

If we wish to share in that same awareness, we must learn to think cosmically, to see everthing in the light of eternity, to recognize the inner and the outer universes, time and eternity, as *one*.

The secrets of the cosmos reveal themselves to us only at the level of cosmic consciousness. That consciousness allows us to perceive the fundamental cosmic dynamisms and organisms behind the visible mechanisms of our space-time senses, and behind these, the infinite Spirit of Life and the universe.

Those who have cosmically awakened realize that everything accessible to human senses and instruments is but the smallest part of the core of the spiritual All-world. That totality, expanding beyond the physical universe, is again part of the divine worlds which in turn belong to a metacosmic reality.

Immanuel *Kant* guessed this when he looked at the wonders of the Milky Way and expressed the thought that "all these immeasurable stellar orders form the unity of a number which in turn is only the unity of a higher combination of numbers. We see the first links of a progressive relation of worlds and systems, and even this first part lets us realize what one should conjecture of the *whole*. Here there is no end but an abyss of real immensity. The wisdom, the goodness, the power manifested here is infinite and, in precisely the same measure, fertile and active; the plan of its revelation must therefore also be infinite and without limits."

Cosmic Consciousness

What makes the awakening to this consciousness such

a happy experience is man's realization of his cosmic origin and future. Man recognizes himself as *a brother of the stars*. Here knowledge becomes wisdom, that wisdom which caused Jacob *Boehme* to confess, "I derive all my knowledge not from books but from my own interior; for heaven and earth, the universe and all life therein, and God himself dwell in the innermost of the soul."

A man or woman who has cosmically awakened and become conscious sees how both his own life and destiny and those of all other beings are directly interwoven with universal events. He feels within himself the breath of the Godhead throbbing through the worlds. He recognizes that *his inmost Self is a spark of the Divine, a child and heir of the universe.*

He knows that no thought blows away with the wind without leaving a trace, that no flower blossoms in vain, that no creature in the universe is lost, because it is connected with all, developing in common to the "Omega Point," the unity of all beings in God.

He is sure that the meaning of the universe is *life* and its law, *love;* that on billions of worlds, as on the Earth, all life is striving for self-unfoldment and Godself-realization. In the physical as in the spiritual universes all is *one:* a cosmocybernetically governed, hierarchically ordered *Whole,* vibrating with and directed by the dynamic creative powers of the Spirit of Life.

Age-old wisdom speaks of Parabrahman or Ain Soph, the immeasurable Suprabeing of the universal Godhead whose visible vestment is the universe and whose Light-thoughts are the individual beings in all the worlds. Even in the meanest and last of those beings the universal Spirit is undivided and present.

At the transfiguration of Jesus "heaven opened" and he saw the Kingdom of God encompassing all worlds in the universe with their billion mansions and, simultaneously, the Spirit of God in the inmost of every being. In the same way, all those who attain cosmic consciousness realize happily that a soul pervades the entire cosmos and that they are one with all life in it.

From then on, they become free and active participants in the cosmic life, while before they were slaves bound to their everyday tasks.

I. *NEW HORIZONS*

If we wish to get a realistic picture of superman of the future, we must switch to a *new kind of thinking,* a new way of seeing. The technico-scientific vision of the futurologists is as insufficient as the merely biological one.

It is only in the psychocybernetic depth view, which does not proceed from external forms and appearances but from the purposive *inner tendencies and potencies,* that the seeds of the future start growing.

Among the great pioneers of the psychocybernetic view of life and the world we count *Meister Eckhart* and *Emerson, Fillmore* and *Sri Aurobindo, Teilhard de Chardin* and other artists of a new mentality, for whom life is eternal progression and the universe a living Whole.

They are no dualists and pessimists but spiritual monists, pan-entheists and *optimists* who, literally, view the development of life as aimed at a cosmic *optimum:* the union with Emerson's "Oversoul," with Teilhard de Chardin's "Omega Point."

They tell us that life and its development cannot be understood statically but only as dynamic phenomena.

In this dynamocybernetic view, the scientific and religious realizations of East and West combine in a new synthesis—in the spirit of unity.

Those materialists who are still in favor of the *static* view believe that the riddles of life have already been solved. Life, they say, is subject to the availability of protoplasm, of albumen, the composition of which is known and can be manufactured artificially.

Life is more than the sum of its organic components. We can only get closer to its secret by considering it from the dynamic psychocybernetic angle.

We know today that the microbuildingstones of both organic and inorganic matter, the elementary particles, are immaterial formations, energy agglomerations, behind which steering potencies may be recognized, in the clearest way, in the organic realm.

The morphologist and vitalist Hans *Driesch* rightly spoke of the "autonomy (self-directing freedom and independence) of *all life,* its insolubility into physico-chemical processes."

Ervin *Liek* reached a similar conclusion, "Behind all matter there is Spirit—and this irrational, metaphysical is what we call *life.*"

Another medical doctor, *Hufeland,* called the world of life the "mysterious veil behind which spirit weds matter." He saw in matter nothing but the building materials with which life is working continuously like an artist, according to specific ideas or ground plans, elaborating even higher forms in the course of aeons.

With ever greater clarity, C.L. *Schleich* stated that the soul is the "inner engineer of all life, who is himself indestructible and part of a higher psychic order which is ultimately grounded in the world soul."

Modern man speaks of the *"inner kybernetes,"* the steering Self or spirit within us, a spark of the All-Spirit and collaborator of the *"cosmic kybernetes"* or God.

Those who deny this Spirit resemble that microbe intelligence of which *Roos* tells the following anecdote:

"At a meeting of those tiny microbes of which there are billions in our body, an especially enlightened microbe requested to speak against the superstition of the age."

'My honorable fellow-microbes, I hope there is not one among us who still holds on to the outdated idea that a being governs our world by his will: this immense red stream of life to which we surrender so readily in order to be carried away to unknown regions of this world; those mighty mountains over there, from which a constant roaring may be heard, and those high vaults above our heads!

Such a ridiculous assumption of a mysterious being, so to speak a *supermicrobe,* a million times larger than we, that is supposed to rule and "animate" this world which in reality has come into being out of itself— I hope you understand and agree that it is unworthy of a thinking microbe to adhere to such a superstition."

All-Harmony

The deeper insights we achieve into the inner plan and hierarchic structure of the realm of life and the *harmony of the Whole,* the more we agree with the philosopher,

"This world in which we live is the creation of an august cosmic Spirit. Evidently, he did not intend to create a finished product, but wishes to give his works the opportunity to perfect themselves in freedom and by their own power, so as to approach more and more the idea of the Creator and to resemble ever more the Spirit of the Whole."

Indeed, in the psychocybernetic depth view the nature and development of life in general, and of man in particular, turn out to be structured according to a grand universal plan that reaches toward the most distant future.

Goethe already saw in our home planet a "nursery" for spiritual beings.

"It would probably have given God little pleasure to compose this coarse world of simple elements, letting it roll along year after year in the rays of the sun, if he had not planned to found on this material basis a nursery for a world of spirits. Thus, he is now continuously active in the higher natures in order to attract the lesser."

From here it is but one step to the comforting realization that "nature is a great *Whole,* complete in itself and supporting itself, in whose infinite circle our human existence is also planned and contained, and in whose immense rotation our small circles move along."

The poet-philosopher Bruno *Wille* had nothing else in mind, "Within you, mortal man, the Eternal is creatively at work. In you, God wants to take form, so that one day perfect wisdom should radiate from you and kindness toward all."

Sure, we human beings of the twentieth century are by far not what we appear to be destined to become—conscious collaborators of the world Spirit; but that we shall be some day.

We are developing steadily, and in present-day *homo sapiens* we already see the forerunner of *homo superior* or *superman* of the future.

II. *The Cosmic Imperative*

Biologists who are still thinking in static-materialistic terms, dream of the artificial generation of man. They hope soon to be able to breed geniuses on the assembly line by influencing and altering genes. A friend of Stefan Georges, the poet L. *Derleth,* made some pertinent comments about those efforts.

> The apes of God are once again searching to
>   counterfeit in their alchemical crucibles
> that which is eternally germinating in the primordial
>   substance.
> And they speak—as though life were but the result

of physical forces,
'Let us create man in *our* image and likeness,
    pulling his spirit from earthly liquid manure.'
Terrible, when foolishness behaves supercreaturally,
    usurping the role of the Creator!
They labor in vain and will never
    enchain the spiritual principle
which is cause, not the product, of matter,
    to the law of gravity."

Man and Machine

We have already seen that science tries to solve this problem from the *technical* side, and we have shown that no *computer,* however perfect, will ever replace man.

It is known that electronic calculating machines, or computers, can already compose music, write poetry, undertake language translations and produce art work.

The magazine "Umschau" (1-70) reproduced some colored drawings made by a computer, the abstract patterns of which were undoubtedly more pleasing to the eye by their symmetry and color symphonies than many a "creation" of hypermodern artists.

They were produced by a novel method of composing abstract patterns by means of a computer-controlled screen developed by John *Mott-Smith* of the Air Force Cambridge research laboratories in Bedford, Massachusetts.

Here again we see that the controlling hand of creative man is indispensable for the production of meaningful and pleasing results.

It is also clear, however, that the combination of the production possibilities of computers with the creative intelligence of man in a new symbiosis leads to new possibilities and the optimum development of the specific human abilities.

How valuable the "symbiosis man-machine" is also in

the economic sector not only becomes evident in automatic language translations but likewise in the production of new industrial materials, in the construction of aircraft parts and many other technical and scientific discoveries.

Of greater importance, however, is the idea and attempt to achieve an improvement and step-up of the cerebral and mental performance of human beings based on the processes at work in computers.

Here we find an indication of entirely *new possibilities for the optimum activation of the creative powers of man,* the increase of his mental efficiency, which will facilitate the step from homo sapiens to homo superior.

With the realization of these possibilities, we act in agreement with the *cosmic imperative* for the carrying out of which man is obviously structured.

In every living thing—most evidently so in man—impulses oriented toward the future are at work, guiding tendencies which, if viewed only superficially, point to an anticipated course of development. A deeper look allows us to conjecture a hierarchically structured cosmic plan of evolution, within which all parts *converge* universally, that is, they meet one another, strive toward one another, reveal a common basis of life and steer purposively toward a homogeneous *Whole*.

Viewed psychocybernetically, life, the world and the cosmos behave as though they were a homogeneous organism: the organ of self-realization of the World Spirit which we call "God."

We can even notice this hidden trend and orientation in our inventions. What, for instance, are our technical achievements but conscious or unconscious imitations of processes created in the organisms ages ago by the formative powers of Spirit—and more subtly and perfectly?

Until now, nature has been man's teacher. But man of the future will go further, realizing ideas that point beyond the realm of matter to the superrealm of Spirit.

On his cosmic course of development, man will put new senses, new organs, new powers and abilities into the service of progressive self-realization.

But just as the world of modern man would be incomprehensible to primitive man, the range of consciousness and breadth of realization of superman of a future age are largely unintelligible to us. We have, however, a sort of vague feeling that we are on the way to the fulfillment of our cosmic task as laid down by the founder of Christianity, "Become ye perfect, as the Father in Heaven is perfect!"

All great minds and teachers of humanity have recognized this *cosmic imperative* and affirmed that it can indeed be realized. "Even the mere will," *Schiller* said, "raises man above the animal world; the moral will, however, elevates him to the Godhead."

To the extent that a man no longer looks exclusively to the outside but is also steadily turning inward, he discovers behind the wonders of the Inner-All his kinship with the Spirit of the Whole and, ultimately, his oneness with it and, through it, his total security.

A human being who feels the cosmic imperative within himself knows that he is forever becoming, growing incessantly with the whole of nature. Added to his feeling of certainty about his infinite future in the consciousness that he is imperishable.

Modern homo sapiens is not the final result of earthly evolution, but only the beginning. In the same way, his next stage of development, that of homo superior or *superman,* is but a further step in the series of upward transformation of human nature. It will be followed in the coming aeons by the levels of the spiritual man, the universal man and the Godman.

III. *THE GROWING REALM*

We know that the universe expands, extending on all

sides like a giant soap-bubble. Similarly, the realm of life expands and, most noticeably for us, man expands.

The more the rate of his growth increases, the more clearly he realizes that he exists in a cosmos of infinite possibilities of which he has up to now activated and realized hardly one millionth of one per cent.

The world in which we live is not static but dynamic. And the more we human beings recognize that we are dynamisms, spiritual force fields with an unimaginable potential of cosmic dimensions, the quicker the transition from homo sapiens to homo superior or superman takes place in advanced types.

Guarantor of this infinite higher development is the divine spark in the core of our being, which is incessantly at work in our physical form.

This "inner man" is a child of the universal Spirit. And, in Goethe's words, "no matter how much he is attracted by the Earth, he lifts his eyes to heaven, searching and longing, because he feels deeply and clearly within that he is a citizen of that realm, the faith in which we are unable to reject or give up. In this presentiment lies the secret of our searching and thinking."

"Why be *human* at all, if you do not strive for the superhuman!" With these words the poet urges us to recognize that "past and present are but the means, while our purpose and goal lie in the future." The reminder of the mystic,

> "You are a part of the All, and not so small
> That you do not carry within yourself the
>   unity of the great Whole,"

is an allusion to the universality of our nature, from the intracosmic depths of which the impulses for progressive perfecting surge.

Here we find an explanation for the cosmic traits in human thought.

Here we also find the certainty of the immeasurable future awaiting us.

In our deepest heart we know, "Out of the universe I come; into the universe I go; thus I am becoming ever more perfect."

Here we find the headwaters of that "cosmic optimism" which sees all development move toward greater perfection and is sure of an infinite future.

Let us try to shed light on some stages of the coming human development by means of a quick-motion device, so that we may "see the mountains of the future world in the morning gold of a sun that has not yet risen for the present generation."

It is an immense idea that is here striving to find expression. But will we succeed in getting pictures of the future world that come close to reality?

Let us become so sure of the future that we realize that our efforts in the past and present are not in vain but form the prerequisite for the future attainment of the noblest goals of humanity.

Cosmic Catastrophes?

"Man will never get that far," the cultural pessimists object, pointing to the possibilities of terrestrial and cosmic catastrophies which could put a premature stop to life on earth. Are they right?

Sure, man has it in his power to destroy *part* of earthly life. But life and reason will ultimately get the upper hand.

Sure, the Earth is aging and neither do the suns in the universe shine eternally. But the most advanced life that exists on the planets of dying suns is then well able to exchange its home for a younger solar system.

The same applies to possible collisions of suns which could endanger planetary life. Given the infinite distances of the suns from each other, collisions are so rare that we men, in the words of the astronomer *Jeans,* must wait about a quintillion years until a star overthrows us.

He adds that we are still walking too much in the gray morning fog of human evolution to have a clear picture of how our world will appear to our successors—the supermen—who will see it in full daylight and that, as far as we can see, astronomy too tells us that there is a future life ahead of us so long that we cannot even imagine it.

But after man has matured into superman, it will take him only a fraction of that time to kick off the earthly dross and "turn to new worlds and life forms."

End of the Earth—Not the End of Life

No matter what the last days of the Earth will look like, spiritual man of that most distant future will at most view the events as a cosmic observer, remaining himself unaffected by them.

When the light of our sun will one day go out as a small red star in the sky and night and cold spread over formerly flowering fields, earthly life will long have left its place of birth—like a butterfly leaving the caterpillar.

The cosmic speck of dust called "Earth" is not the grave of mankind but the cradle and first home of the human race. From its base, mankind will go on a pilgrimage into the immensities of the universe, in search of new places for living, working and perfecting itself.

There are no adequate grounds for assuming that humanity will one day share the fate of the *saurians* and, because of senility, yield its rule to other creatures, such as ants or giant amoebae.

Just man, who in comparison with the armor-plated reptiles is much weaker but endowed with spirit, will withstand all cosmic changes of a biological, meteorological, climatic and cosmic nature. He will adapt himself to them in the course of millions of years, survive through endless ages, becoming more perfect as time goes on. Rudiments of his next level of development, that of superman, may already be seen in contemporary man.

IV. *Homo Superior*

> "Have respect for the image of man
> and remember that therein,
> however concealed,
> the seed of all that is highest
> grows for some future morning."

What *Hebbel* sensed and what we may see in faint outline even today is *superman of the psychocybernetic Age,* growing out of present-day man.

The term "superman" is not to be interpreted in the sense of Nietzsche's "Herrenmensch" (lordly man, master man), but in its original meaning of "homo superior," that is, the more perfect spiritual man, as *Herder, Hippel, Jean Paul* and, above all, the Rosicrucian *Johann Valentin Andreae* dreamed of and aspired after.

Let us now shrink the millennia to seconds with the quick-motion device of the soul and let our first stop be superman!

To begin with, we shall see with some surpise that he does not in the least resemble the caricature made of him by futurologists who assume that, in the course of ten thousands of years, man will lose his hair covering, his teeth, his muscular strength and much more, degenerating into a kind of intelligent beast, such as H.G. Wells' "Mars-men" who consist only of an abnormally large head and weak, antennae-like rudiments of arms and legs.

On the outside, homo superior will hardly differ more from contemporary man than we differ from Neanderthal man, compared with whom *we* are already "supermen."

Inside, however, enormous changes have taken place which have a transforming effect upon life and the environment.

Even the nobler form of superman's head shows that the development of his brain, that ingenious psychocybernetic installation, is to a small degree quantitative but to a larger degree qualitative. In other ways, too, his inner structure differs essentially from ours according to his more refined psychic constitution.

As a *psychoeugenicist,* who knows how to use his body and life in an unimaginably perfect way, he has hormonized and harmonized his body to the utmost in regard to beauty, health and vitality.

As a *psychocyberneticist,* who deploys the power of the mind through the indwelling soul and the creative spirit, he fully mobilizes a multitude of latent powers and talents and extends his efficiency on all sides by systematically activating his positive hereditary factors.

He sees in his body a living microcosm, woven out of light and power, which is in constant communication and communion with the macrocosm and performs wonders of transformation. Since, in addition, the idea of "Tat tvam asi," this—all living things—is yourself! includes animals, he considers a vegetarian diet natural sunlight food. He helps the higher animal forms by arousing and advancing their consciousness.

Being a *mental energy field,* his life process is not a caloric but a bioelectric and biocybernetic phenomenon. He is a master of the art of exchanging vital energy, by which he largely prevents or mentally removes tension and sickness.

Medicine and surgery have been replaced by psychurgy which effects the desired psychosomatic changes through mental action.

In a similar way, the predominance of spirit also affects the *technical,* economic and social sides of his life.

Superman's Environment

The ideal symbiosis of creative man with innumerable

positron servomechanisms, which science is already attempting today and which will be developed to the utmost by superman, obviously serves the maintenance and advance of life, all life.

In this connection, the wonderworks of the *biotechnology* of superman appear to be living embodiments of divine creative ideas which serve to control life and the environment from within, deepening the harmony of man with nature, with the universe and the Spirit of Life.

We shall see no metropolis inimical of life and encompassing continents. We shall see no towering or abysmally deep stony deserts throbbing with greed and noise and a hectic chase after success. Instead, we shall see an immense green sea of woodland parks, interspersed with bright dwellings. They are places of biotechnical and mental creativity, the results of which serve the progress and prosperity of all, because they are founded on reverence for life and the spirit of universal friendship.

In contrast to contemporary man, superman will be an ingenious "heart" thinker. We envision a spiritually united mankind governed by a spiritual and cultural aristocracy whose members are valuated and selected as preliminary stages of the *spiritual man* of a still later future.

The "struggle for life," which today still determines man's thinking and doing, will be "debrutalized" by superman and raised to the higher level of a free and friendly competition of all forces for the benefit of the whole.

In comparison with modern man, homo superior is in every respect a self-determined artist and master of life, for whom every thought and every work is *religion:* manifestation of his harmony with the whole of life, an opportunity for further perfection and conscious progress to that higher level to which he feels destined: the *spiritual being* of coming aeons.

FROM SUPERMAN TO UNIVERSAL MAN

I. *Even the most Distant Future lies Within Us.*

One of the most important discoveries of our time concerns the stratification of consciousness: below the collective unconscious, we find the layer of the *superconscious* interconnecting all beings. Still deeper, there stretches the more inclusive layer of *universal and God-consciousness*. This experience has so far been granted to only a handful of men. When it does occur, it opens up new dimensions of Reality to those who have followed the way inward to the end.

While ego-consciousness is sense- and timebound, the superconscious and Allconscious tower into the suprabeing region of timelessness. Thus, they reach into that which is latent within us as the *future*. It is still inaccessible to our ego-consciousness, although it is the *present* for the deeper layers of consciousness.

This enables us to have isolated visions of the cosmic way of mankind, at moments when we succeed in touching the plane of cosmic consciousness for a brief span.

Then we realize that the future is not as it is seen by some science fiction writers. It is not a world of intelligent cyborgs and humanoid superrobots who have made man superfluous. Rather, it reveals the gradual higher development of contemporary man until he reaches the level of spiritual and universal man.

Man and the Universe

Although we cannot spend much time in surveying the separate stages of humanity's cosmic evolution, the few glimpses we catch by the soul's quick-motion device furnish interesting data.

In the beginning, science had established a few space stations. They were good launchpads for visits to the stars and also served as astronomical observatories. Subsequently, the moon, Mars and the other planets were used as cosmobiological laboratories and they became the first stations in the intergalactic communication network.

In the meantime, great progress had been made on earth in the unification of mankind. Man did finally attain planetary maturity, a prerequisite and first step toward cosmic maturity. From then on, he was able to establish contact and secure positive cooperation with alien life forms beyond the boundaries of the solar system, from where his vision roamed freely to the next stellar realms.

It was also at that time that science discovered that the speed of light is no ultimate limit. The discovery of a modification of the force of gravity and, subsequently, of the primal energy, enabled man to achieve velocities in comparison with which the speed of light creeps at a snail's pace. Now man could soar to distant solar systems where he discovered a diversity of starstudded planetary worlds. Their number increased to infinity with later intra- and extragalactic travels.

Since time stopped nearly altogether for the cosmonauts, space travel deep into the universe entailed a prolongation of life covering thousands of years, and this longer life span was used in many different ways.

It is remarkable that in spite of those achievements,

man did not forget his home and community on the Earth and that the dynamism of his soul as well as his openness for the wonders of cosmic life increased with the expansion of his space travels.

Plurality of the Worlds

One of the first surprises for superman of the first intergalactic space travel Age is the discovery of a *cosmic communication network* that has existed for millions of years. It is set up on a telepathic and empathic basis and the realization that the universe is much more multi-layered and immense than anyone could imagine.

Superman of the future has some glimpses into the hierarchic structure of cosmic life. But only *spiritual man*, who succeeds him at a still later stage and after experiences of cosmic consciousnesss, becomes an active partner in these universal communications and exchanges of information which connect him with life forms of whose constitution and power contemporary man cannot even dream.

Among these, we count spirit entities who people cosmic space. This space is by far no "vacuum," but is filled with a profusion of energetic, plasmatic and vital currents and agglomerations of forces of which the visible heavenly bodies are only *one* kind of manifestation.

There is one thing, however, for which we look in vain in that period: those images of cosmic wars of which many science fiction writers dream and who, in addition, tend to transpose earthly conditions to other worlds—a mentality that has so far excluded mankind from cosmic intercommunication.

From Superman to Spiritual Man

Examined from the vantage point of *superman,* contemporary human life, science and activity appear prehistoric.

To *spiritual man* awakening to cosmic maturity, we humans of today look like shapeless preliminary stages of true human nature.

And yet we contain the seed, the predisposition for this spiritual and universal man of future millions of years.

What do we see when we focus the bioscope of our quick-motion device on these future descendents of ours?

First, spiritual man, in his godlike corporeality veiled in a soft auric light, appears to us like an embodiment of the ideal of everything good and beautiful in a perfect body-soul unity.

If, as *Schleich* said, to be a genius means to be born with a few billion more neurons than the average person, spiritual man can be considered the ideal image of both the man of genius and the master of life.

He is in such direct conscious contact with his body that he "talks" to his organs and cells, sending them information and directives and ensuring their intelligent cooperation.

As a *metabiologist,* he evidently masters the science of influencing all living matter, not to mention his dominion over lifeless matter. Let us now take a closer look at him.

II. *Spiritual Man of the Future*

Already in our time, science has recognized that man's organism, including his brain, is undergoing a gradual change toward higher development. From the viewpoint of natural science, there is nothing against the assumption that *new senses* will arise in man of the future and that hitherto unknown dimensions of reality will open up to him.

We see this prediction come true in *spiritual man of the future,* while realizing that this development exists already as a seed in the psychosomatic constitution of contemporary man and is noticeable in isolated cases.

In the phenomena of telepathy, clairvoyance, clair-audience, psychometry, telekinesis, etc., which are today still relatively rare, psychobiological possibilities and senses come to the fore which are as fully developed in spiritual man as our normal seeing and hearing.

Then, science will know for sure what it can only conjecture today, namely, that the *brain* is not the only center of sensory activity. In addition to the *heart* and the *pineal gland,* the *solar plexus* in particular, as well as other networks of interlacing blood vessels and nerves, and last not least the skin, are switchboards for multiple interconnecting sensory activity.

The Senses of Spiritual Man

Although it looks as though the entire organism of spiritual man were a single sense organ, it is unmistakable that besides the brain as sender, the ganglionic wonderwork of the *solar plexus* as receiver is a center of mental and spiritual sensory activity.

Schleich called it intuitively the "All-nerve" or "universal organ," by which man is rhythmically connected with events and life in the cosmos. Here spiritual man is in touch with the mental impulses of other beings as well as the vibrational fields of things.

His sense for radiations is equally well developed.

Just as it is a long way from the light-feelers of primitive animals—a spot of pigment reacting to light and dark—to the organ of vision of modern man, so it is a long way from the latter to the electro-optical radiation sense of spiritual man, which covers far greater areas of the ether frequency than our today's vision.

To him, the cosmos is full of life and activity. To him, nature is "an Aeolian harp, the sounds of which are in turn notes of higher chords in his own soul." Like Merlin the Sage, he hears "voices that are mute for others . . . ." To his sensitive ears, the secret chords in the realm of the living, the inner sounds of nature and the harmonies of the cosmic spheres are life's songs of joy.

When he concentrates his vision and thoughts on a distant star, he senses, like the legendary astromants of antiquity, its nature, condition and constitution and the kind of life that exists on its planets.

To his *allopsychic senses,* cosmic space is not only filled with radiation and energy impulses from stars, nebulae, galaxies, quasars, etc., but to a much larger extent with innumerable thought waves, mental and spiritual vibrations and currents of information and, behind it all, the vibration of the Divine.

He is able to answer foreign impulses and get in touch with civilizations of other worlds through the language of thoughts which bridges cosmic distances in no time at all.

At the same time, he disposes of other senses. Although they are still in the process of unfolding, they point to the coming of a yet higher type of man at whose realization the "inner kybernetes," the divine bio-architect in man, is already at work.

Eudynamicist and Psychurgist

The richness of spiritual man's inner life corresponds with his environment, which surpasses everything imagined or dreamed of by futurologists.

Spiritual man masters in a superb way what we are today aiming at under the term *"psychodynamics,"* that is, the practical application of the "atomic energies of the soul," the fully activated power of thoughts, belief and volition.

He is in command of the techniques of *telekinesis* as well as *telebuly* (remote effects achieved by the will) directed toward both living beings and the intelligent servomechanisms of his epoch.

In addition, we find that he can exchange information with his equals beyond the limits of space and time, at a mental speed unimaginable for us. Together, they can solve problems and cause chain reactions on a planetary scale by coordinating their plans.

The ethics of spiritual man corresponds with this direct mental communication and collective focusing of the will. Negative thoughts, selfish conduct harmful to the community have become impossible, since they would automatically be neutralized by the environment through positive mental radiation.

All in all, spiritual man is seen as a *eudynamicist* and *psychurgist,* that is, a master of the art of life-promoting deployment of force, actualization of thoughts and ingenious productivity.

He works deliberately with the formative powers of the soul, the inner organizers and architects of all life, for the purpose of progressive self-perfecting. Simultaneously, he makes the best use of the servomechanisms of his time, which are controled by corresponding thought waves.

But as perfectly as he may dominate his environment, what is of importance to him is the higher-dimensional world of spiritual Reality where he lives and works as consciously as we humans are now living on the material plane.

To him, the "Here" and the "Beyond" are *one* world, and death is for him but a passage through a gate from one room to the next.

We men of today would feel this state of affairs as a continual intoxication of life, and we would hardly be able to stand it. For spiritual man, however, it is a matter-of-course attendant phenomenon of his spiritual alertness and potency.

In spite of all this, he is fully aware that he is only a first step in the progress toward a yet higher type: universal man and the Godman of a still more distant future.

III. *Universal Man of the Most Distant Future*

Looking with a quick-motion device at that far distant

future when *universal man* has made his home on countless space worlds, we realize that we humans of today are set up for this development. Among others, *W. Bösche* recognized this fact,

"Man is a Proteus in regard to endurance, provided he is allowed sufficient time to change and adapt slowly to external conditions and threats to his existence; he will then be able to achieve the most ingenious adaptations."

In fact, during his space explorations in the course of aeons, man adapts to the varied cosmic conditions, armoring himself more and more effectively against all dangers to his life in space and the various heavenly worlds with their different living conditions.

Simultaneously, it would seem that the transformation of spiritual man to universal man results in a rejuvenation of the human race.

In the soundlessness and weightlessness of space, superman became aware of his task to develop into universal man.

It is at this stage when the old divine command, "Subject the Earth to yourselves," expanded into the *cosmic imperative,* "Rise up to the stars and prove yourselves to be children of the universe!"

In compliance with this imperative, *universal man* learned to create heat and cold fields around him as he needed them and to change still uninhabited space worlds into homes for aspiring spirits.

His organism adapted to space radiation as well as the gravity and biological conditions of the large and small space worlds, first by technical, then biotechnical, psychobiological, and finally mental means and methods.

Universal man expanded the diversity of spiritual man's activated senses by a number of *space senses* which allowed him to feel more and more at home in the universe, enabling him to meet all requirements of his cosmic surroundings in an optimum way.

Since he activated the ninety percent of the gray cells

or neurons of the brain that are still unproductive in contemporary man, he possesses a power of comprehension and wealth of knowledge which make him look like a god in our eyes.

World Traveler and World Transformer

He has become a world traveler who is at home everywhere and in continual mental contact with all areas of the universe.

He knows that he is connected with the inhabitants of the millions of planets of our home Milky Way, as much as with those of the neighboring galaxies, and he cooperates with them in many ways in the higher development of the various life forms.

Everywhere his omnipresent senses see light, motion and activity: Spirit in action.

It is with special love, however, that he takes care of his relations with those higher galactic communities which observed terrestrial life as far back as when man was just testing his latest discoveries, the wheel and fire.

The more the radius of his life extends, the deeper is his reverential admiration for the immensity of the universe and the Spirit of Life behind it.

The more spectacular the circumference of his knowledge and activity grows, the more numerous are his points of contact with the region of the still unexplored and the metacosmic realm of the World Spirit. Wherever he is, he feels equally close to the World Spirit, with whom he is connected with every impulse of love and in whom he feel totally secure.

Whatever he undertakes in cosmic cooperation, however, is obviously based on the spirit of reverence for life, oriented toward the free and independent higher development of all beings.

He is fully aware of what Teilhard de Chardin sensed in our Age, that everything visible in the universe exists for *Spirit* and is a means for the unfoldment and self-realization of Spirit, not just for the *human spirit* but for the divine spark in *all* beings in the universe.

For all are "inseparable from the cosmos in birth and maturing." All are children of the cosmos. All are destined to reach the final goal of perfection and oneness with God in the course of their evolution.

Universal man progresses from spiritual man's All-communication to *cosmo-communion.* He is conscious of his inner relationship with all life at the four corners of space. He knows that life is older than the visible universe, since it belongs to a higher reality by its nature, even if it is bound to planetary forms of existence during its cosmic unfoldment.

To him, the universe is a *biodynamic whole:* a single life form permeated by Spirit and pulsated through by God, as it were, the visible organism of the invisible Godhead.

Of course, he is still bound to his body, but he is already in touch with far more developed beings who no longer require a body cover and no longer collaborate in the development of life as organisms but as energisms.

In the same way, he knows the higher-dimensional spirit worlds as well as the infinity of his own inner universe and the bliss of oneness with the Spirit of the Whole.

Morgenstern's words have become true for him, "God attains the highest level as man; the most developed, perfected man is simultaneously a supreme moment of bliss for God."

To him, self-realization, the goal of universal evolution, is God-self-realization. Religion is *life* for him, and the entire life, *religio.*

But even if he knows that he has reached a climax in the process of God's embodiment in human form, he feels that the Godhead holds forever a future in store for him that surpasses infinitely anything he has so far attained.

IV. *Godman and the "Omega Point"*

Viewed from a sufficient height, as a *Whole,* the world shows the characteristics of a mass of consciousness in motion. After 500 million years of life and 500,000 years of humanity, the Earth continues to organize itself. Its psychic temperature rises. This is what Teilhard de Chardin recognized.

Rightly so, for the Earth and the universe tend to converge. All life, for the sake of which the universe exists, is striving for optimum cooperation, for common perfecting and universal unity.

If we direct the bioscope of the soul's quick-motion device beyond universal man to the Godman of the most distant future, we become aware of the symbolic character of this life and recognize, in the light of eternity, the gradual *self-revelation of the Godhead* in the cosmic evolution.

From that viewpoint, the Godman resembles the "prodigal son" who returns home into oneness after aeons of wanderings through the worlds.

Ultimately, he returns from the four corners of the universe to the depths of his own *inner universe,* there to experience the bliss of his at-one-ness with the *Eternal,* before whom all time is a nothingness, and the endless host of universes and meta-universes but a thought, a breath.

He feels the breath of the Godhead, which reveals itself in the becoming, decaying and regeneration of creatures and worlds.

And he sees his own path through the worlds during immeasurable periods of time, his eternal *upward* within the progressive spiritualization of matter and the divinization of spirits.

Before his eternity-eye, the totality of all thisworldly and otherworldly, three-dimensional and multi-dimensional realms of life is revealed. He sees the ceaseless passing from here to there and from there to here of all beings in the service of their self-realization as *one single life*.

To him the word applies, "A *man*, a pilgrim awakened to Being, ends; a *God* begins his course."

In him, mankind's two ideals of immortality merge and become embodied in a sublime synthesis:

The ideal of one kind of man was "to be put before ever greater tasks in the course of his future evolution, to work as active co-creator of the Eternal, to collaborate mentally in the education of other beings, to direct planetary and solar systems in their evolution. This is what the great *Goethe* desired and considered man's supreme achievement.

The other kind of man, like *Meister Eckhart*, was especially interested in spiritual evolution or involution; the possibility to grow spiritually, rising to ever greater visions, to immerse with increasing bliss ever deeper into God's splendor, and to share in the divine plenitude."

Omega

The Godman reaches that focal point of cosmic convergence which Teilhard de Chardin has called the "Omega Point" in which he sees all life currents of the cosmos merge in the highest unity of absolute suprabeing.

The cosmic evolution reveals itself to his visionary sight as a spirit-directed striving of all worlds and beings toward the absolute *cosmic megacenter*.

Indeed, from the beginning everything in the universe is moving toward perfect unification, with growing consciousness, intensity and speed.

Christ's demand, "Be ye therefore perfect, as your heavenly Father is perfect" is met in full in the Godman, so that he can say with Christ, "I and the Father are *one*."

The divine spark in him is one with the primordial sea of Light of the Eternal. He shares directly in the universal energy field of consciousness. In him, the consciousness of every being is as vividly present as his own. "Tat tvam asi."

To him, all beings in all the worlds are a sole *All-organism,* permeated by the same Spirit, and *every* individual in it possesses the full plenitude of the universal powers, like a living God-cell.

In accordance with Christ's words, "In my Father's house are many mansions," the substantial *unity of all* god-awakened universal beings coincides with an infinite *individual manifoldness.*

The Godman is happy in the knowledge that *unification* does not mean either uniformity or disintegration of the individuality but, rather, differentiation in the highest degree, which knows no opposites but only unison and harmony.

The bond uniting the infinite individual diversity of the Godmen is the divine *power of love* at the basis of all evolution. In it, equal partnership in the divine essence is combined with the absolute freedom of those entities who have achieved self-realization.

The Meaning of Existence

Has the Godman reached the end of cosmic evolution when he has arrived at the "Omega Point"?

As far as definite knowledge may be obtained on this point in the depths of one's own Self, the Godman does not yet represent the ultimate but is himself, in turn, a new beginning.

When the "Omega Point" is attained, it is simultaneously an "Alpha Point." It is the beginning of a new metacosmic evolution, which may well include myriad times more wonders than the cosmic evolutionary levels from primitive man to the Godman, leading beyond the cosmocrats and divine beings into the blazing All-heart of the universal Godhead.

And what is the meaning of this immense evolutionary cycle from primeval being to universal being, from primitive man to the Godman and beyond?

The way of all evolution points from the finite to the infinite, from the temporary to the eternal, from the earthly to the cosmic, and from the human to the divine and beyond.

In the light of eternity, behind every recognizable goal and meaning, deeper, more abysmal, goals come into view, goals that cannot be fathomed, not be made out.

To quick-motion vision, the most obvious meaning of the universe is *life,* and the most obvious task of the stars, to be nurseries for spiritual beings: training stations for the spiritualization of matter and the divinization of spirits.

Behind this, the deeper meaning of the drive forward, the drive for the *perfecting* of all living things, is concealed. In turn, this drive is accompanied by a pull upward, to *convergence:* to ever more harmonious collaboration of all beings in the universe.

We find that the divine power of *love* is the ultimate driving power at work behind everything.

Simultaneously, we see in the light of love that the fulfillment of the highest task of all life, "to become perfect as the Father in heaven is perfect" is not the end of evolution but the beginning of a new *metacosmic becoming,* determined and directed by the primordial law of eternal love.

In it, we touch the deepest discernible meaning of the Whole. In it, life returns to its primary source.

The highest experience of the perfected Godman—the direct experience of God—is oneness with the Spirit and the power of eternal love. In it, he sees revealed *that God is love, and that love is God.*

THE COSMIC WAY OF MANKIND

First American Edition — 1975

THE COSMIC WAY OF MANKIND by K.O. Schmidt was published by CSA Press, Lakemont, Georgia. Approximately one thousand and five hundred copies of this first American edition were printed by CSA Printing & Bindery, Inc., Lakemont, Georgia from 11 Point Times Roman on Hammermill's Lock Haven Natural Offset and bound in Holliston Roxite Pyroxylin Impregnated binding fabric. The end papers are Strathmore Americana. Design format by Robert H. Brannan.